A Dad's Prayers *for* His Daughter

Praying for Every Part of Her Life

Rob and Joanna Teigen

Revell

a division of Baker Publishing Group
Grand Rapids, Michigan

Published by Revell
a division of Baker Publishing Group
P.O. Box 6287, Grand Rapids, MI 49516-6287
www.revellbooks.com

Printed in the United States of America

Library of Congress Cataloging-in-Publication Data
Teigen, Rob.
    A dad's prayers for his daughter : praying for every part of her life / Rob and Joanna Teigen.
        pages cm
    Includes bibliographical references.
    ISBN 978-0-8007-2262-3 (pbk.)
        1. Fathers—Religious life. 2. Intercessory prayer—Christianity.
    3. Daughters—Religious life. 4. Girls—Religious life. 5. Prayers. I. Title.
    BV4529.17.T455 2014
    242'.8421—dc23   2013039637

14 15 16 17 18 19 20   7 6 5 4 3 2 1

"Praying for your daughter is one of the most important things you will ever do in your life. I have seen God do amazing things in my daughter's life by committing to praying for her. If you're a dad with daughters, you're going to want to read this book."

—Mark Batterson,
author of the *New York Times*
bestseller *The Circle Maker*

"All daughters want to be 'seen' by their father. They long to know they are special and loved by him. Rob and Joanna Teigen's prayers in this book will help you see your daughter in a new way and do the most powerful thing: love her through your prayers."

—Chris Fabry,
author; host of *Chris Fabry Live!*

"Rob and Joanna Teigen have written the ideal book to help fathers pray for their daughters. They've covered virtually every area that a daughter needs prayer coverage in. Then they've given dads the perfect words to use. Want to be a better dad? Pray for your kids. This book will help."

—Rick Johnson,
bestselling author of *That's My Son, That's My Girl,*
and *Better Dads, Stronger Sons*

"Is there any sweeter legacy that a man can leave for his girl than the knowledge that her daddy prayed for every area of her life? Rob and Joanna Teigen give dads the tools they need to make that hope a reality. I love their warmhearted but practical approach to equip men in their pursuit to be the dads they want to be."

—Kathi Lipp,
author of *Praying God's Word for Your Life*
and *21 Ways to Connect with Your Kids*

"*A Dad's Prayers for His Daughter* works on so many levels. Well-chosen Scripture and heartfelt prayers make this an invaluable resource. But the hidden benefit is how Rob and Joanna have opened a surprising window into your little girl's world. The future is undeniably filled with moments of blessings and brokenness, love and loneliness, the need for courage and the need for compassion. And dads must be prepared. These inspired pages will help caring fathers guide their daughters through every season of life."

—Jay Payleitner,
speaker; bestselling author of
52 Things Kids Need from a Dad

"Our girls are inspired when they know they are loved, hear encouraging words, and know we are praying for them. Rob and Joanna Teigen have crafted a great book to help dads succeed in these vital areas with their daughters. I highly recommend this book!"

—Bill Farrel,
author of *Men Are Like Waffles,
Women Are Like Spaghetti*;
www.love-wise.com

To our daughters,
Emma, Leah, and Anna
You are loved!

Contents

A *Word* from *Rob*

Prayer goes where a parent can't. It softens hard hearts, enlightens darkened minds, and guides lost souls. Prayer is a parent's way of taking matters into God's hands.

Will Davis Jr.[1]

Everybody knows me as the dad who likes to have fun. I've written joke books for kids and a whole book of daddy-daughter date ideas. My wife rolls her eyes every time I get rowdy with the girls when I'm supposed to be settling them down for the night. My favorite time of the day is when I walk in the door after work and head straight out to the trampoline to jump around with the kids. We go to concerts, have Starbucks dates before school, and demolish the kitchen every Christmas baking cookies together.

I spend all this time with my kids because I love them. They make me laugh. They're my favorite people! But I also invest the time because I believe their relationship with me is crucial to their future. If they feel loved and cherished by me, they won't be as likely to meet their needs in the wrong places. If we're comfortable and open with each other, I can share my faith and speak truth into their lives. Most of all, the love they receive from me is their first taste of the love of God himself.

I realize, though, that no matter how much time we spend together, I can't control who they will ultimately become. All the instruction, advice, and protection I give won't ensure that all will go well in their lives. No matter how often I take them to church and have family devotions at the dinner table, I can't make them embrace my faith in God and live for him.

This is why I have to put my daughters in God's hands. It encourages me to know that even though I'm not a perfect dad, God will always be a perfect Father. I don't always know what's best for my girls, but God does. The best thing I can do is bring my daughters and their needs to him in prayer. It's not our last-ditch effort to make things come out okay—it's the *first* thing we should do because it invites the power of God into their lives.

Sometimes, though, it's hard to know exactly how to pray for a daughter. I can't always relate to her emotions. She has struggles and experiences that I'm not always aware of. I'll see an attitude or perspective that needs adjusting, but I don't know what to say. It can be hard to know whether she needs more limits or greater freedom. That's why we wrote this book—to offer some insights about parenting and prayers that put words to the concerns dads feel for their girls.

This book is a tool to help you as you bring your daughter to the Lord in prayer. It may be useful to pray through a prayer every day or every week, or to pick it up when a specific topic is on your mind. Take time to read and meditate on the Scriptures included with each prayer so God can speak to you through his Word. Don't feel limited by what's written on the page—the Lord is eager to hear your needs and praises in your own words too.

I'm encouraged as a dad when I see God responding to the prayers of other men I know. Several prayers and stories are included in the book that show how other men have prayed and seen God respond in their daughters' lives.

Prepare to be changed as you commit yourself to praying for your daughter. God will give you greater strength and wisdom in your parenting. Your faith will be stretched as you wait on him to work in her life. You'll find yourself letting go of your own expectations and asking God what *his* priorities are. You'll become a stronger parent as you experience God's influence in your own life. You'll begin to release your dreams and hopes for your daughter as you realize God has had plans in mind for her life since before the creation of the world! You'll find more grace for her mistakes. More patience in waiting for her to mature. More courage in knowing the Lord will go through every challenge by her side. More delight in her individuality. And more gratitude as you see she is truly a gift from God just for you.

It is a privilege to share this book of prayers with you. May you be blessed as a father as you bring your daughter's needs before the Lord. I pray you will find a helper and friend in him that you've never fully known before. God bless you and your family.

Rob

A *Word* *from* *Joanna*

I am so very grateful that I have a praying husband. Knowing that he brings our needs to God so faithfully gives me security and makes me feel loved. It reassures me that we're not walking this parenting journey alone. The burden of responsibility for our kids can feel too heavy to bear on our own.

What I've noticed as we've prayed over the years is that God does just as much work in changing *me* as in caring for my girls. I know a lot of us moms tend to worry. We work ourselves up over their grades, health, manners, organizational habits, and social lives. Our emotions run high over their weaknesses, and it can be hard to celebrate their successes when so many fears are constantly running through our minds. When Rob and I pray for our daughters, it settles me down. I put all of my concerns in God's lap and am able to let them go.

My girls know how to push my buttons too. They know if they roll their eyes when I'm talking I'm probably going to lose it! It's really difficult to see our daughters struggling with bad attitudes. Again, when I'm tempted to get angry about their choices, prayer lets me release them to God's control. He gives me patience and understanding. I'm able to see the big picture instead of fixating on minor issues. He reminds me of all the many, many things I enjoy in my girls and the privilege it is to be their mother. He rekindles my joy and fills me with hope for the future. Basically, God makes me a better mom when I pray.

Prayer also keeps a lot of tension out of our marriage. If I'm looking to Rob to "fix" our girls when they mess up, he starts feeling pushed (okay, nagged) about how he should handle things. When we pray and trust the Lord for wisdom and help in raising our kids, then I can relax and be thankful that Rob is parenting them God's way instead of mine.

We've seen God move through our prayers to change our daughters' lives—we've seen them grow in confidence, discover their talents and passions, and come to know the Lord as their Savior. We're in the trenches just like you, raising our children the best we can and praying God will hold on tight to each of us. My hope for you is that you'll find him to be all you need as you parent your own daughter. Discover how near he is to you. He wants to bless you both as you reach out to him.

Joanna

— 1 —

When She Needs
God's Salvation

Jesus said to her, "I am the resurrection and the life. The one who believes in me will live, even though they die; and whoever lives by believing in me will never die. Do you believe this?" "Yes, Lord," she replied, "I believe that you are the Messiah, the Son of God, who is to come into the world."

John 11:25–27

See that you do not despise one of these little ones. For I tell you that their angels in heaven always see the face of my Father in heaven. What do you think? If a man owns a hundred sheep, and one of them wanders away, will he not leave the ninety-nine on the hills and go to look for the one that wandered off? And if he finds it, truly I tell you, he is happier about that one sheep than about the ninety-nine that did not wander off. In the same way your Father in heaven is not willing that any of these little ones should perish.

Matthew 18:10–14

Loving God,

Thank you for my beautiful daughter. I know that she is your creation, planned before the beginning of time. You know every little detail about her. You cherish her and desire her salvation, so she can live her life in you and can spend eternity in your presence.

Reveal yourself to my daughter. Work in her heart so she can respond to your love. Give her an unshakeable faith in Jesus—believing he is your Son sent to seek and save the lost.

Without your salvation she has no future and no hope. She won't be able to comprehend the truth of your Word, which directs our steps and teaches us how to live. She won't receive the gift of your Spirit, who brings comfort, wisdom, and help as we make our way through this confusing world.

Claim my daughter as your own. Write her name on your hands. Put your seal on her and write her name in your book of life. Give her eternal life so no one can snatch her out of your hand.

Thank you that my daughter and I can grow in faith together. Put words in my mouth that explain your message of salvation clearly, in terms she can understand. Use me as your messenger of hope as I share my own faith story and live for you every day. Help me to abide in you and live faithfully so she sees your power in me.

I trust you, Lord, to work in my daughter's heart and bring her to full belief and trust in you. Thank you for the future we can look forward to—enjoying your glorious presence together, forever. Amen.

— 2 —

When She's My Treasure

Behold, children are a gift of the Lord, the fruit of the womb is a reward.

Psalm 127:3 NASB

Great is the Lord and most worthy of praise; his greatness no one can fathom. One generation commends your works to another;

*they tell of your mighty acts. They speak of the glorious splen-
dor of your majesty—and I will meditate on your wonderful
works. They tell of the power of your awesome works—and I
will proclaim your great deeds. They celebrate your abundant
goodness and joyfully sing of your righteousness.*

Psalm 145:3–7

*Every good and every perfect gift is from above, coming down
from the Father of the heavenly lights, who does not change like
shifting shadows.*

James 1:17

Lord,

You did a "mighty work" when you created my daughter.
She has been a "good and perfect gift," a greater treasure than
I could ever have imagined. Thank you for loving me so much
that you would bless me with this precious girl.

My daughter is the most amazing gift from you that I can
imagine. Becoming her father has been a life-changing experience—a *me*-changing experience. She has brought love
and humor, creativity and joy to our home. Parenting her has
taught me so much about myself and even more about you,
my heavenly Father.

May I never take my daughter for granted. I don't want
to lose sight of the gift she is when guiding or correcting her
becomes a challenge. I know that she was created by you and
specially chosen to be my very own child. You have purposes
that I have only begun to catch sight of.

Open my eyes to see your unique handiwork in her mind
and personality. Use me to bring out her confidence and joy.
Teach my heart to treasure her. Guard me from selfishness so
I don't become wrapped up in my own interests and squander
the time you've given us to be together.

Help me to cherish my daughter the same way that you devote yourself to me. May I imitate your faithfulness, wisdom,
and unconditional love. Fill me with your compassion and

understanding. May I never stop praising your name for the gift of my daughter. Amen.

— 3 —

When She Feels Inferior

For you created my inmost being; you knit me together in my mother's womb. I praise you because I am fearfully and wonderfully made; your works are wonderful, I know that full well. My frame was not hidden from you when I was made in the secret place, when I was woven together in the depths of the earth. Your eyes saw my unformed body; all the days ordained for me were written in your book before one of them came to be.

Psalm 139:13–16

The LORD your God is with you, the Mighty Warrior who saves. He will take great delight in you; in his love he will no longer rebuke you, but will rejoice over you with singing.

Zephaniah 3:17

Lord,

You know how my daughter struggles with insecurity about her physical body. The world fills her eyes with so many false ideals—flawless skin, hair, weight, fashion—that are impossible for any girl to live up to. She sees the young women on TV and the models in magazines and wonders, *What's wrong with me that I don't look that way?* Sometimes that question can shake her to the core.

I pray that the truth in your Word will put her insecurities to rest. Help her to believe when you say she is wonderfully made and that her body is a miraculous gift. Help her to see that her life is no accident because you had her in your mind's eye for all of time. May your deep love and devotion be a comfort when she's brought down by other voices saying, "You're not good enough."

As her dad, give me wisdom with my words. Use me to build her up and affirm the beautiful creation she truly is. Guard my mouth from speaking any criticism that could feed the self-doubt she's already feeling. May she experience your love through me as I cherish her inner and outer beauty.

You say that perfect love drives away fear—may your great love bring peace to her heart. May she discover your wonderful grace and acceptance. Let us worship you as you rejoice over us. Amen.

— 4 —

When She Covets More

What causes fights and quarrels among you? Don't they come from your desires that battle within you? You desire but do not have, so you kill. You covet but you cannot get what you want, so you quarrel and fight. You do not have because you do not ask God. When you ask, you do not receive, because you ask with wrong motives, that you may spend what you get on your pleasures.

James 4:1–3

Father God,

You know our hearts—we want what we want, and we want it now! It causes a lot of conflict in our home when our children compete for possessions, being first, or the attention they desire. Everyone wants to be heard first, to have more *stuff*, and to feel like they're on top.

I pray that you would soften my daughter's heart. Calm her passion to be first and to have what she's craving at the moment. Give her the humility to put others first rather than herself. Give her patience as she waits for answers from me and from you when she makes a request.

Please bring peace into our home. May we have a loving, giving, sharing household that is free from selfish fighting and arguing. Teach us to value one another over material things. Keep us from "murdering" each other with hateful words and behavior when we feel cheated out of what we feel we deserve.

Teach us the difference between real needs and the cravings of our flesh. May we become more and more prayerful, bringing our dreams and desires to you. Make us patient and thankful as we wait on you to receive what's best for each of us.

Use me as a voice of gratitude in our home. Keep me from faultfinding and complaining. Rule my heart so I can live out an example of contentment before my daughter's eyes.

Thank you for being our source of every good thing. May we count our blessings and live in peace with one another. Amen.

— 5 —

When She's Afraid

The Lord is my light and my salvation—whom shall I fear? The Lord is the stronghold of my life—of whom shall I be afraid? . . . For in the day of trouble he will keep me safe in his dwelling; he will hide me in the shelter of his sacred tent and set me high upon a rock. . . . I sought the Lord, and he answered me; he delivered me from all my fears. . . . This poor man called, and the Lord heard him; he saved him out of all his troubles. . . . Taste and see that the Lord is good; blessed is the one who takes refuge in him.

Psalms 27:1, 5; 34:4, 6, 8

Father,

A child has so much to be afraid of—strangers, the dark, getting lost, embarrassment or failure at school, rejection by friends, and the disapproval of her parents. Some children even have to fear violence, hunger, and being alone in the world.

Please comfort my daughter by your power and strength. Help her to truly believe in your promises to protect and care for her. Give her faith to know that you hear her prayers and are waiting to comfort all her fears. May trusting in you give her confidence to face every person and situation that comes her way.

As her dad, may I never be a source of fear in her life. Keep me from out-of-control anger that will destroy her trust in me. May I be a strong protector of her body, her mind, and her emotions. May I be gentle and kind by your Spirit. Give me wisdom to know when to set boundaries for her safety. Give me courage to say no to people or experiences that could place her in harm's way, even if she doesn't agree or understand.

Sometimes she is timid or fearful of new opportunities. Help her to step out and try new things even if it's uncomfortable at first. Keep fear from taking control of her decisions. Give us both the wisdom to know if her doubts are based simply on emotions or real threats to her well-being.

Thank you for being our stronghold and shelter. You are our hero! Amen.

A Dad's Story

grew up in a Christian home, and for that I am eternally grateful. My grandfather Fred was an incredible man of God who served as a pastor in Jacksonville, Florida. As Christians, my mom and dad have both prayed for me and with me my whole life. When I was a very lost teenage boy, God answered their countless prayers for my salvation and more. Jesus saved me and placed a unique calling on my life that I'm still seeing unfold. He called me to himself as well as into vocational ministry as a sixteen-year-old young man.

As I look back, I can see God's sovereign hand of providence guiding me each step of the way. Today, I'm the daddy of a little girl, Tovah (three), and a little boy, Jude (twenty months), and I have the greatest privilege of helping my wife, Jana, with dinnertime, baths, story time, songs, prayers, and bedtime. I say this is a privilege because I genuinely believe that snuggling by the fire, talking about kitties, and tracing squares and circles in an activity book is holy work. God prefers to be called *Abba* (Daddy) by his children (Gal. 4:6; Rom. 8:15), and so it's out of an overflow of my relationship with him that my children directly benefit. As I put Tovah to bed every night, I pray for several things like her health, that God will save her very early on in life, that she will spend her entire life knowing that Jesus loves her, and that she will share his love with others.

Every night, I pick and pray for a different decade of my daughter's life, all the way up to one hundred years old. For example, I pray for Tovah that in her preschool class next year, another child who loves Jesus will befriend her. I'm praying that in her elementary school years God will give her a soft heart just like Jesus has toward all kids from all races and socioeconomic backgrounds, and those with physical challenges, and that she will not fall into small-mindedness. Other nights, I pray for her teenage years. I pray that God will use her as an example of what it means to have character that is given to her by Jesus and not just follow whatever some crowd says is cool. I'm asking God to give her a deep love for the truth during high school and to walk in the light as he is in the light. I pray for her early college years that she'll not only have a soft heart and solid Christian character given by the Holy Spirit but that she'll also have an incredibly sharp mind that can reasonably defend and effectively share her faith in the university setting, with the hopes of more people meeting the Jesus she loves and worships.

I have dreams and goals for my kids and want to provide the best life possible for them, from home, to school, to whom they date and marry, as well as their careers. However, my prayers are not simply a means for me to get my way. Ultimately, my prayers for Tovah are an act of worship as I hand her back to our great God who loves her more than I ever will, has greater plans than I could ever imagine, and will care for her long after I'm in glory. I will be her daddy for a matter of days. God is and will always be our heavenly Father forever and ever. Therefore, I'm speaking to him often about his (my) baby girl, Tovah Kate.

Alex Early,
pastor of preaching and theology,
Living Stones Church, Reno, Nevada

— 6 —

✷ When She Thirsts for God

As a deer pants for streams of water, so my soul pants for you, my God. My soul thirsts for God, for the living God.

Psalm 42:1–2

Jesus answered, "Everyone who drinks this water will be thirsty again, but whoever drinks the water I give them will never thirst. Indeed, the water I give them will become in them a spring of water welling up to eternal life."

John 4:13–14

Lord,

We are all born thirsty. Our hearts are dry and lifeless and we never feel satisfied. We dig our own wells as we search for water—material things, popularity, a perfect appearance, success at school or work—and our thirst just intensifies.

Please create in my daughter a desire for you and you alone. Teach her that she can only find satisfaction in you. Help her to find you, to know you personally, and to walk with you every day of her life.

Allow my daughter to experience your living water. Give her a taste of how wonderful you are so she will reach for you again and again. Help her to seek you with all her heart and discover that the answer to all of her longings lies in you alone.

May I have a deep yearning for you as well. Don't allow me to ignore my thirst when I've become distant from you for any length of time. Keep me from going back to the old wells I made before I knew that *you* were the life I was looking for. May I love your Word and never end the day without connecting with you in prayer.

Keep us from hoarding your water for ourselves. Let us freely share the hope we've found in your gospel. Use us as bearers of your message to the world.

Thank you for your salvation. I praise you for the eternal life we have in you. Amen.

— 7 —

When She Needs Peace

How good and pleasant it is when God's people live together in unity!

Psalm 133:1

Finally, all of you, be like-minded, be sympathetic, love one another, be compassionate and humble. Do not repay evil with evil or insult with insult. On the contrary, repay evil with blessing, because to this you were called so that you may inherit a blessing.

1 Peter 3:8–9

Blessed are the peacemakers, for they will be called children of God.

Matthew 5:9

Father,

You know how girls can be! They bicker, gossip, pick favorites, and break off into groups that one day let you in and the next day shut you out.

I pray that my daughter will be able to rise above the crowd and be a peacemaker. Please keep her words free from gossip or from tearing others down. Allow her to be a leader by setting an example of kindness and humility. May she set a standard of friendliness and acceptance in her school and circle of friends.

Give my daughter the courage to reach out to kids who have been insulted or pushed to the margins. Help her to encourage anyone around her who feels lonely or insecure. Give her wisdom to know how to handle the petty arguments and gossip that she finds herself in the middle of.

Let my daughter be slow to take offense and quick to forgive. Fill her with a gracious spirit that refuses to hold a grudge. As far as it depends on her, may she live at peace with everyone (Rom. 12:18).

For my part, help me to set an example of peacemaking by the way I interact with the people in my life. May I consistently seek unity with my wife, my children, my coworkers, my church, and my extended family members. Don't let my pride keep me from getting along with others. Keep my speech from any slander that would hurt others and set a poor example for my daughter.

Thank you for sending Jesus to make peace between us and God. May that peace flow through us to everyone we meet. Amen.

— 8 —

When She's Angry

Like a city whose walls are broken through is a person who lacks self-control.

Proverbs 25:28

The one who has knowledge uses words with restraint, and whoever has understanding is even-tempered.

Proverbs 17:27

In your anger do not sin": do not let the sun go down while you are still angry. . . . Get rid of all bitterness, rage and anger, brawling and slander, along with every form of malice.

Ephesians 4:26, 31

But you, Lord, are a compassionate and gracious God, slow to anger, abounding in love and faithfulness.

Psalm 86:15

Lord,

You know how in our weakness we can lose our temper! We have those days when everything seems to go wrong, and it's easy to take out our frustration on each other. You've witnessed the ugly words and behavior that my daughter and I have shown when we unleash our anger in the heat of the moment.

However, you challenge us not to be mastered by our emotions. We don't have an excuse that can cover the harsh, angry words we say. Please teach us by your Spirit to be self-controlled, to keep our tempers in check, and to be full of mercy rather than rage.

Examine my heart and show me the root of my anger. Cleanse me of selfishness and pride that demand my own way.

Break any generational patterns of anger and abuse—you make me a new creation and are my true Father.

If I have failed to correctly train my daughter, please forgive me. Give me wisdom to know how to guide her in being patient and able to express her thoughts and emotions in a respectful way. Help her when she's tempted to be overcome by feelings that rise up so quickly and lead to sin.

You know what frustrates my daughter the most, and you know the root of her anger. If she is reacting to not having her own way, give her humility and a heart of obedience. If others are provoking her with insults and disrespect, may she find her value in you so her self-image isn't shaken. If fatigue or stress is affecting her ability to cope, help her find rest so she has strength to face the day. Soften her heart so she can respond to challenging people and situations with compassion instead of retaliation.

Make our home a haven where each one of us is safe—emotionally and physically. Give us the humility to ask for forgiveness when we wound each other. May we have the wisdom to take a "time out" if we need to cool down. Put people in our lives who give us a right perspective when we're tempted to overreact. Allow us to love each other so much that we never end the day without making peace between us.

Thank you for your mercy and grace. We fail every single day but you never give up on us or "let us have it." May I be a father like you—loving, patient, self-controlled, and full of love for my child. Amen.

— 9 —

When Her Life Is Set Apart

Do not be yoked together with unbelievers. For what do righteousness and wickedness have in common? Or what fellowship can light have with darkness? What harmony is there between Christ and Belial? Or what does a believer have in common with an unbeliever? What agreement is there between the temple of God and idols? For we are the temple of the living God. As God has said: "I will live with them and walk among them, and I will be their God, and they will be my people." Therefore, "Come out from them and be separate, says the Lord. Touch no unclean thing, and I will receive you." And, "I will be a Father to you, and you will be my sons and daughters, says the Lord Almighty."

2 Corinthians 6:14–18

Almighty God,

Thank you for making us yours. You have brought us into the light and made us your temple. You call yourself our Father and welcome us into life with you. You live with us, walk with us, and promise us an inheritance as your children.

Those are amazing truths, but somehow it's still easy to fall in with the world around us. We forget that we have been set apart. We pattern our thoughts and behavior after the people around us instead of Christ. Remind us that by your power we have all that we need for life and godliness (2 Pet. 1:3).

Keep us from loving what the world loves! Help my daughter to escape the traps of chasing after money and popularity. Give her a desire to please you with modesty and humility. Make her courageous so she can resist temptation and stand for what's right.

Protect my daughter from those who would lead her away from you. Keep her from discouragement when she's criticized by unbelievers who don't understand her beliefs or choices. Bring friends into her life who have committed their way to you. Surround her with believers who can encourage her to remain faithful. Protect her heart, saving her love for a husband who lives fully for you.

Give my daughter kindness and compassion for those who don't yet know you. May they see your light in her life and be drawn to find out who you are.

Thank you for being our loving Father. Amen.

Her Relationship with Her Dad

One of the greatest things about fatherhood is being the most important man in my daughter's life! But I've met many dads over the years who are completely oblivious to how much their daughters really need and desire to have a close relationship with them. Kevin Leman says it well in his book *What a Difference a Daddy Makes*:

> A woman's relationship with her father, more than any other relationship, is going to affect her relationship with all other males in her life—her bosses, her coworkers, subordinates, sons, husbands, brothers, pastors, college professors, and even Hollywood movie stars. . . . There is not a single relationship that isn't indelibly stamped—for good or for ill—by the man known as daddy.[2]

I've met other dads who *have* grasped how important a strong relationship is to their daughter's life, but they just don't know where to start. That's where I was when we had our first baby girl. I was completely captivated by her and wanted to be the best dad I could be. I had read and heard how important our relationship would be to my daughter's growth and development, but after growing up in a home with all boys I had no idea where to begin.

If you're in either one of these camps, let me start by saying that nearly every dad has been there at some point. We just don't want to give up before we even begin to work on a closer connection with our daughters.

I remember talking to a dad over lunch one day, and the topic switched to a book my wife and I were writing at the time, *88 Great Daddy-Daughter Dates*. He had one boy and one girl. He told me he knew he should be doing more to develop a relationship with his daughter, but it was hard to know how. He described how it was easy to connect with his son—they would wrestle on the floor for a few minutes or go outside and throw the ball around, and the boy's relational needs were basically met. With his daughter, however, it was more difficult. I encouraged him that it was never too late to begin. While my daughter is little, she still has plenty of time to spend with me. She doesn't think she's too cool to be seen with me in public. There's lots of fun, simple ways to spend time together and create memories. And when we make those moments happen over and over when she's small, we develop a bond that will last when she's older and her needs are more complex.

If your daughter is older and you haven't been able to cultivate that close relationship over the years, take heart. No matter how distant she feels or how little you understand each other, you're still the most significant man in her life. Don't fall into the belief that it's too late for you. Examine your history to see where you have let her down, and find the humility to go to her and ask for forgiveness. No matter how she responds, she'll always remember your words and willingness to take responsibility for your actions as a father. If she doesn't seem eager to spend time with you, find other ways to express that you're interested in her life. Leave a funny card on her dresser. Slip a gift card into her coat pocket. Find thoughtful ways to serve her, like washing her car or charging her phone. Talk to your friends about how proud you are of her when you know she's in earshot. And most of all, lift her up in prayer every day. Ask God for insight into how to win her heart.

Maybe you have a wonderful relationship with your daughter. She shares her hopes and dreams with you, she runs to meet you when you get home from work, and she gives you more hugs and kisses than you can count. That's awesome! But whether you have a fantastic relationship with your daughter or it's a work in progress, you can entrust everything to our perfect Father. He loves us faithfully and unconditionally and is a God of second (and third, and nine-hundredth) chances.

Experience the power of God in your relationship with your daughter through prayer. Go to him for everything—your communication, your time together, working through conflict, ways to build her up—and most of all, praise him for blessing you with the gift of your daughter. He wants to express his love and care for her through you, so invite him in and see all that he will do.

Rob and Joanna Teigen

– 10 –

When She's Rejected

You have heard that it was said, "Love your neighbor and hate your enemy." But I tell you, love your enemies and pray for those who persecute you, that you may be children of your Father in heaven. He causes his sun to rise on the evil and the good, and sends rain on the righteous and the unrighteous. If you love those who love you, what reward will you get? Are not even the tax collectors doing that? And if you greet only your own people, what are you doing more than others? Do not even pagans do that? Be perfect, therefore, as your heavenly Father is perfect.

Matthew 5:43–48

Lord God,

You know what it feels like to be hurt and rejected. You know the pain of being ignored, ridiculed, and wounded in the most horrifying ways. We read the story of Jesus's betrayal and death, and we grieve the injustice he suffered.

Because of that, I take comfort in knowing you can relate to my daughter's suffering at the hands of others. She may experience the lies and gossip of her classmates. She may get turned away by the group of girls she most wants to belong to. A friend may misunderstand her and react in anger, and my daughter may find herself alone. She may have to watch a reward that is rightfully hers being given to someone else. People will disregard her property at times by damaging it or losing it.

It seems too difficult to obey when you say to "love your enemies and pray for those who persecute you." But I do want to be your son, and I long for my child to be your daughter. Give her the strength to put aside her selfish desires and give your grace to everyone in her life.

Do your perfecting work in her heart. Guard her from keeping a count of every wrong she suffers. Don't allow her mind to dwell on the ugly words of others, imagining the perfect sarcastic remark she could have spoken in the moment. Give her the strength to forgive whether the other person is sorry or not.

Guard my heart so I never push my daughter away through my words or actions. It's impossible for her to be perfect, and I want to accept her as she is. She won't always measure up to my expectations, but I never want her to have to earn my love. May I give her grace, just as you give to me, when she struggles or fails in any way. Use my faithfulness to give her a glimpse of how perfect and truly devoted to her you are.

Fill us with compassion for everyone. Show us how to reach out to others, no matter how unlovable or "unlikable" they are. And in this way, may we be your light in the world. Amen.

– 11 –

When She's Finding Her Treasure

Do not store up for yourselves treasures on earth, where moths and vermin destroy, and where thieves break in and steal. But store up for yourselves treasures in heaven, where moths and vermin do not destroy, and where thieves do not break in and steal. For where your treasure is, there your heart will be also. The eye is the lamp of the body. If your eyes are healthy, your whole body will be full of light. But if your eyes are unhealthy, your whole body will be full of darkness. If then the light within you is darkness, how great is that darkness! No one can serve two masters. Either you will hate the one and love the other, or you will be devoted to the one and despise the other. You cannot serve both God and money.

Matthew 6:19–24

Heavenly Father,

This world is full of amazing things! And all the advertisements, shopping centers, and catalogs make it seem like everything we see should be ours. Please guard our hearts from loving the treasures of this world. Keep us from coveting the latest technology, every current fashion on the racks, the latest model at the car dealership, and the neighbor's home that always has better curb appeal than ours.

Guard our minds from pride that makes us feel entitled to having whatever we want. If we earn a reward or are blessed with greater income and responsibility, let us praise you for equipping us with the energy and talent to accomplish it.

Protect my daughter from finding her identity in mere things. Keep her from getting caught up in the "who has what" comparisons among the kids at school. Don't allow her security or self-worth to become based on her possessions. Beyond that, don't allow her to judge the value of others by what they do or do not have.

It's easy to get so hung up on disappointments about what we can't afford that we miss the greatest treasure of all—you! May we be so satisfied with your presence in our lives that nothing else can compare. Help us to remember that all of our work here on earth isn't about acquiring more *stuff* but building your kingdom for eternity.

We want to be mastered by you alone, not by the material things we see with our eyes. Satisfy all of our cravings with yourself, we pray. Amen.

– 12 –

When She's Going through a Storm

That day when evening came, he said to his disciples, "Let us go over to the other side." Leaving the crowd behind, they took him along, just as he was, in the boat. There were also other boats with him. A furious squall came up, and the waves broke over the boat, so that it was nearly swamped. Jesus was in the stern, sleeping on a cushion. The disciples woke him and said to him, "Teacher, don't you care if we drown?" He got up, rebuked the wind and said to the waves, "Quiet! Be still!" Then the wind died down and it was completely calm. He said to his disciples, "Why are you so afraid? Do you still have no faith?" They were terrified and asked each other, "Who is this? Even the wind and the waves obey him!"

Mark 4:35–41

Almighty God,

You know the storm my daughter is experiencing. She has fears about her circumstances, that they will overwhelm her and be more than she can handle. She feels alone in her struggle, and sometimes she wonders if her prayers make a difference. Sometimes she tries just to put on a brave face, as if struggling means she's weak or a failure.

We can be like the disciples, believing you are sleeping and oblivious to what we're going through. Or a storm comes along and we put every effort into "bailing the boat" and solving our problem by ourselves. It isn't until our efforts are exhausted and hope is gone that we finally run to you for help.

Teach my daughter and me to go to you in every struggle. Show how you are near and full of love for each of us. You are strong and kind—powerful enough to rescue us and loving enough to want to! May this particular hardship my daughter is going through become a story of your goodness in her life.

Give us strength to believe that you use every difficulty for our ultimate good. You don't want us to just survive; you want to show your power and bring perfect peace. You promise to teach us perseverance, to grow our faith, and to display your glory. May my daughter find joy, knowing this temporary pain will deepen her knowledge of you.

Use me to help and encourage my precious girl. Guard her heart from doubt. Strengthen her faith so she is more sure of you than anything in the world. Thank you for your power and love. Amen.

– 13 –

When She Needs to Tell the Truth

Better a little with righteousness than much gain with injustice.

Proverbs 16:8

No harm overtakes the righteous, but the wicked have their fill of trouble. The LORD detests lying lips, but he delights in people who are trustworthy.

Proverbs 12:21–22

Do not lie to each other, since you have taken off your old self with its practices and have put on the new self, which is being renewed in knowledge in the image of its Creator.

Colossians 3:9–10

Father,

I pray that you would guard my daughter's mind, actions, and words from any kind of dishonesty. As a child, it can be tempting to use lies to avoid consequences, impress others, avoid responsibilities, or even tear others down.

I pray that my daughter would have the courage to face the consequences of her choices, even if they're difficult. Help her to receive correction with humility instead of making up excuses. Give her the courage to confess her mistakes instead of bending the truth to avoid discipline.

Please teach my daughter to place her identity and reputation in your hands. Relieve any pressure she feels to embellish her talents or achievements to impress others. Give her a loving heart that can celebrate the gifts and accomplishments of her siblings and classmates, even if it means she isn't always the center of attention.

Give my daughter a sense of satisfaction in her work, whether it's homework assignments, chores, or serving others. Guard her from using deceit to cover up any lack of responsibility. If she fails to finish what's required of her, let her own up to her actions and work wholeheartedly in the future.

I pray that my daughter would never lie about others in order to harm their feelings or reputation. May her words be filled with kindness and encouragement for everyone in her life. Keep her lips from malicious gossip and any kind of insult or slander. Make her a blessing as she walks in honesty and truth.

Allow me as her father to model integrity in every area of my life. Guard my speech from exaggeration, false excuses, repeating rumors, or outright lies. May you, our Truth, make us righteous by your Spirit. Amen.

– 14 –

When She Needs Wisdom

Blessed are those who find wisdom, those who gain understanding, for she is more profitable than silver and yields better returns than gold. She is more precious than rubies; nothing you desire can compare with her. Long life is in her right hand; in her left hand are riches and honor. Her ways are pleasant ways, and all her paths are peace. She is a tree of life to those who take hold of her; those who hold her fast will be blessed.

Proverbs 3:13–18

The fear of the LORD is the beginning of wisdom; all who follow his precepts have good understanding. To him belongs eternal praise.

Psalm 111:10

If any of you lacks wisdom, you should ask God, who gives generously to all without finding fault, and it will be given to you.

James 1:5

Father,

Every day we face all kinds of choices and decisions. How do I tackle that project or assignment? How should I spend my free time and manage my money? Who will I choose to spend time with? How will I handle that disagreement with someone? What goals should I set for my future? How should I protect or discipline my daughter? How will I handle the temptations that come my way?

My daughter and I don't have the wisdom it takes to do the right thing in every situation. Whenever we try to run our lives on our own we make a mess of things. Without your wise counsel and guidance we are lost.

Please give my daughter your wisdom. Show us *your* dreams for her future. Reveal your best plans for her time and money. Give her insight into choosing the right friends, the way to make peace with others, and her own errors that need repair. Show her how to resist temptation and identify which sins are tripping her up.

As a dad, give me your wisdom about when to allow her freedom and when to rein her in. Counsel me as to when to be firm and when to show some grace. When I'm tempted to be too harsh or apathetic, teach me the best means of instructing

39

my child. Prompt me to set boundaries when her well-being is at stake.

Show my daughter that you are her source of wisdom. May she learn even now as a young person that she can go to you with any questions or uncertainties. Let her trust in you rather than her own opinions and impulses. Give her ears to hear your counsel, that it may speak more clearly to her heart than any other voice.

Thank you for your kindness and your compassion on our confusion and foolishness. Thank you that there's no "dumb question" when we ask you for wisdom! Your constant mercy and goodness are a comfort as we face the decisions that come our way. Amen.

− 15 −

When She Needs Courage to Live for God

Have I not commanded you? Be strong and courageous. Do not be afraid; do not be discouraged, for the LORD your God will be with you wherever you go.

Joshua 1:9

So we say with confidence, "The Lord is my helper; I will not be afraid. What can mere mortals do to me?"

Hebrews 13:6

Dear friends, do not be surprised at the fiery ordeal that has come on you to test you, as though something strange were happening to you. But rejoice inasmuch as you participate in the sufferings of Christ, so that you may be overjoyed when his glory is revealed.

If you are insulted because of the name of Christ, you are blessed,
for the Spirit of glory and of God rests on you.

1 Peter 4:12–14

Lord God,

You describe your children as "foreigners and exiles" in the world (1 Pet. 2:11). You say we should expect to be misunderstood, turned away, and even abused by those who have rejected you.

We can grow weary, though, of feeling like the odd man out. People don't understand why we don't enjoy the same entertainment, join in the gossip, chase after the same material things, or fight to come out on top. They think it's ridiculous to "waste" time at church when we could relax or sleep in. Sometimes we get accused of being self-righteous when we hold ourselves to a different standard.

It's difficult for my daughter to feel different from the other kids at school. She feels pushed and pulled about her modesty, her outlook on boys and dating, what kind of respect she should show adults, her language, what movies to watch, what music to listen to, and how to treat other kids.

Sometimes it seems my daughter is bending to the pressure to fit in. Give her the courage to "be strong and courageous." Help her to hold fast to her identity as a child of God, rather than letting the world define who she is. May she be encouraged when she experiences criticism—it's a sign that your Spirit truly lives in her heart. May she find hope in the promise of your blessing each time she's put down for living for you.

Use me as an example of faithfulness and courage. Keep me from making compromises that weaken my allegiance to you. Show me how to encourage my daughter when she's tired or discouraged. May our family continually build each other up. May our home give a sense of belonging to other believers who come through our door.

Thank you for never leaving us alone in this world where we just don't fit in. Your hope and your presence help us to hold on. Amen.

A Dad's Story

A few years ago at a Men at the Cross event in Phoenix, Arizona, I met Samuel Rodriguez. He is the leader of the National Hispanic Evangelical Association. From the time he was a small child, his dad prayed over him daily. After Samuel shared his story with me, I immediately implemented his dad's prayer into our home. I never leave home or allow my kids out of the car without praying a version of that prayer over them: "Father, cover them home in the blood of Jesus. Protect them from evil. Fulfill your purpose in their lives."

My daughter Corynn is convinced that she's never leaving home. At age seven, she made up her mind that Mom and Dad take such great care of her that she'll just stay.

But she knows I'll have none of that.

One of the hardest questions Corynn has ever asked me is, "Dad, who do you love more, me or Mom?"

Ouch! Naturally, my first response to a question like that is to act like I didn't hear the question or to squint my eyes as though I didn't understand it. She has me wrapped around her little finger.

"I love your mommy and you both," I say gently, "but God wants me to love Mommy in a different way. Your mommy and I are together for life in a covenant relationship. We will be together until one of us goes to heaven or Jesus returns. But you, Corynn, will not be with us forever. You will one day leave our home and start a family of your own."

Corynn is quick to reply, "I want to be with you and Mommy forever."

"You can't be with us forever, Corynn," I say.

Corynn knows that she is the princess and her mom is the queen. Corynn will never be my queen, but I will show her every day how a queen should be treated. On the day of her wedding, she will become another man's queen.

As tears form in her eyes, she glares at me and says, "I am going to college online and staying home forever. You can't make me leave." While I must admit I like the sound of that from a tuition standpoint, I need her to know that separation from Mom and Dad is a sign of health and maturity. She will need to leave home one day.

There's a very important verse in the Bible that speaks to parenting in preparation for marriage: "That is why a man leaves his father and mother and is united to his wife, and they become one flesh" (Gen. 2:24). The King James Version uses the word *cleave* to convey being united. In other words, the bond between husband and wife is to be stronger than the bond between parent and child.

I've taught my kids a definition of maturity based on Genesis 2:24 and it's simple: "You will not be with Mom and Dad forever, so plan accordingly." Amen.

From the time God spoke Genesis 2:24 and through the first several thousand years of human history, kids grew up, became adults, and left home. Starting marriage well requires leaving home. Cut the strings. Love and honor your parents, but call home less, buy your own clothes, work out conflict in your marriage without your parents' meddling, seek the input of your spouse over that of your parents, and never ever compare your spouse to a parent.

I love when I am approached by a mom at a wedding and she says, "I don't feel like I'm losing a son today, but I feel like I'm gaining a daughter."

I usually respond with, "Nope, you are losing a son."

One day, I will stand at the back of a church with my princess. At the front of the church will be our friends and family. We will walk down the aisle and I will hand her to a young man, her prince. There I will bless her, cut the strings, place her hand in his, and say, "Father, cover these two in the blood of Jesus.

Protect their marriage and family from evil. And fulfill your purpose in their lives."

Ted Cunningham, founding pastor of Woodland Hills Family Church in Branson, Missouri; author of *Fun Loving You*, *Trophy Child*, and *Young and in Love*; coauthor of four books with Dr. Gary Smalley

– 16 –

When She's Falling into Addiction

Don't you know that when you offer yourselves to someone as obedient slaves, you are slaves of the one you obey—whether you are slaves to sin, which leads to death, or to obedience, which leads to righteousness? But thanks be to God that, though you used to be slaves to sin, you have come to obey from your heart the pattern of teaching that has now claimed your allegiance. You have been set free from sin and have become slaves to righteousness.

Romans 6:16–18

My eyes are ever on the Lord, *for only he will release my feet from the snare.*

Psalm 25:15

Father,

There are so many pleasures in this world that can trap my daughter. In the right context, food, sex, money, success, relationships, and entertainment are blessings from you. In our weakness, however, those things can become addictions that hold us in slavery to their power.

I pray that none of the blessings or experiences of this world will replace you in my daughter's life. May you be her greatest delight. Help her to find her satisfaction and security in you so her heart doesn't crave a substitution.

Give my daughter strength and self-control. Help her to find moderation in her habits and purity in her actions. Give her a grateful heart that worships you rather than the blessings you provide. If there is anything in her life right at this moment that is becoming a snare, please give her release and escape.

Allow me to live as an example of freedom to my daughter. Reveal to me any areas where I am out of balance—pouring my passion and attention into something for the wrong reasons. May she see me as a "slave to righteousness" with my eyes "ever on the LORD." Give me discernment to see any areas in which my daughter is falling into bondage. Soften her heart to receive my insight, and the counsel of your Spirit, so she can walk in freedom again.

I praise your name for the hope we find in you. For "if the Son sets you free, you will be free indeed" (John 8:36). Amen.

– 17 –

When She's Worried

Don't ever worry and say, "What are we going to eat?" or "What are we going to drink?" or "What are we going to wear?" Everyone is concerned about these things, and your heavenly Father certainly knows you need all of them. But first, be concerned about his kingdom and what has his approval. Then all these things will be provided for you. So don't ever worry about tomorrow. After all, tomorrow will worry about itself. Each day has enough trouble of its own.

Matthew 6:31–34 GW

Do not be anxious about anything, but in every situation, by prayer and petition, with thanksgiving, present your requests to God. And the peace of God, which transcends all understanding, will guard your hearts and your minds in Christ Jesus.

Philippians 4:6–7

Lord,

Whenever I sit down to balance the checkbook, look over my daughter's grade report, have my cholesterol and blood pressure checked, have a disagreement with my wife, or see the violent events on the news, it's easy for me to become anxious and worry. It's hard to face an uncertain future where struggles and crises can happen outside of our control.

I know this is a struggle for my daughter as well. She wonders if she'll succeed, if kids will like her, if she'll be smart or pretty enough, and if her hopes and dreams will come true. Sometimes she worries about pleasing me too.

I pray for peace for both of us. Teach us to trust you and put all our burdens into your hands. Give us faith to believe that you will keep your promise to care for us. Use me to point my daughter to you when she's falling into stress and anxiety.

Help us to have your priorities. We can put our own temporary troubles ahead of concern for your kingdom and the needs of others. We get so distracted by material concerns that we ignore a lost world that is perishing without you. We care more about our comfort than our obedience. We want quick gratification instead of the discipline of waiting patiently for you to act in our lives.

Teach us to be faithful in prayer and to know your peace. Guard our hearts and minds from the foolishness of worry. Thank you for your wonderful promises that give us hope. Amen.

– 18 –

When She's Proud

All of you, clothe yourselves with humility toward one another, because, "God opposes the proud but shows favor to the humble."

1 Peter 5:5

Do nothing out of selfish ambition or vain conceit. Rather, in humility value others above yourselves, not looking to your own interests but each of you to the interests of the others. In your relationships with one another, have the same mindset as Christ Jesus: Who, being in very nature God, did not consider equality with God something to be used to his own advantage; rather, he made himself nothing by taking the very nature of a servant, being made in human likeness. And being found in appearance as a man, he humbled himself by becoming obedient to death— even death on a cross! Therefore God exalted him to the highest place and gave him the name that is above every name, that at the name of Jesus every knee should bow, in heaven and on earth and under the earth, and every tongue acknowledge that Jesus Christ is Lord, to the glory of God the Father.

Philippians 2:3–11

Father God,

The world pushes us to have an "all about me" attitude about everything! We want to be the best, come in first, and have our way in every situation. We can refuse to wait for anything and expect everyone around us to gratify all that we desire. We get impatient if we have to wait in line, get stuck in traffic, or even just have to put up with a slow download on our computer.

Please work in my daughter's heart to create patience and humility toward others. Keep her from becoming so self-absorbed that she ignores the well-being of those around her. Don't let her step on others to get ahead or to please herself. Teach her thoughtfulness, consideration, and generosity.

Help me to set an example for my daughter of courtesy and servanthood. Give me wisdom to speak in an honoring way about family members and coworkers. Keep me from becoming self-centered as a dad, ignoring my daughter's needs by getting wrapped up in my own concerns. Let me live before her as someone who cares for the poor, surrenders my own preferences for others, and seeks to be a blessing.

Keep us from any kind of boasting or showing off. May we be humble and obedient in every situation, just as Jesus surrendered to you in everything. And through our humility, may we be the hands and feet of Jesus to everyone.

May you be glorified! Amen.

Her Blessings

The ultimate measure of a man is not where he stands in moments of comfort and convenience, but where he stands at times of challenge and controversy.

Martin Luther King Jr.

I know what it is to be in need, and I know what it is to have plenty. I have learned the secret of being content in any and every situation, whether well fed or hungry, whether living in plenty or in want.

Philippians 4:12

As a father living in a land of plenty, I want to be able to give my daughter good things. Just like Jesus said, "Which of you, if your son asks for bread, will give him a stone? Or if he asks for a fish, will give him a snake?" (Matt. 7:9–10). We know how to give our children what they need. We wouldn't dream of withholding food when our daughter is hungry or a warm coat on an icy winter day. Our fatherly instinct to provide is an integral part of who we are.

I want my daughter to have the best of everything. I usually assume that the very best thing for her is comfort and blessing. Of course I don't want a lazy child who sits around and waits for every luxury to be handed to her on a silver platter. But I do want her to have good health so she can work and play hard. A strong mind to learn and succeed academically. Talents to achieve and attain success. A great personality and social skills so she presents herself confidently and is well liked. Financial prosperity to enjoy the material things the world can offer.

Unfortunately, when I pray for all of these blessings it can contradict what God wants to do in my daughter's life. In his wisdom he may provide challenges, weaknesses, and loss to grow her faith and teach her a greater dependence on him. I was recently visiting a friend who is battling cancer. She quoted the verse I mentioned above and said, "I think sometimes we're asking for the stone when we think we're asking for the bread." This friend went on to say how she was finding cancer to be God's bread for her. I was amazed to be sitting next to my dear friend as she sat on a hospital bed taking chemotherapy treatment into her veins, saying joyfully that "this is God's bread for me!" Through the uncertainty of her illness, she was encountering God in powerful ways as he met her in the middle of her pain.

That is the kind of faith God desires all of his people to have, including my daughter. I know that I slip into praying for her to have a light and easy life, thinking I'm asking for "bread." But God wants more than anything else to have a close, personal relationship with my daughter in which she trusts him completely. If he answers every prayer of mine that asks for blessings, she might become so consumed with enjoying the gifts that she leaves the Giver behind. She may become caught up in pursuing her dreams instead of her Savior's face. She may confuse mere happiness with the true joy of satisfaction in God alone.

I'm slowly finding the courage to pray that God will never give my daughter comfort in any area of life if it will cost her closeness to him. Sometimes I even have to pray that a reward or accomplishment be delayed so she can learn to wait and depend on him. There are times that coming in first would be the worst thing that could happen, because it could stir up pride and hinder her love for others.

Statistics show that although we live in one of the wealthiest countries in the world, our nation has some of the highest rates of depression, suicide, and fear. Clearly money doesn't buy happiness! My daughter will find true peace and satisfaction only in the Lord. If she looks to find it in money, relationships, or success, she'll always end up disappointed. God is big enough to take my daughter's pain, mistakes, and inadequacies and use them as blessings in her life if her eyes are fixed on him.

I need the Lord's help to keep me from giving outside the bounds of his will. He knows when a gift or offer of help will do her good or end up fostering ingratitude or a lack of initiative. It comes up in a myriad of ways every week—should she save her allowance for what she wants to buy, or should I open my wallet? Should I stay over her shoulder while she works on her assignment or let her push through on her own? Will a helping hand in cleaning her closet be an act of kindness or keep her from learning to stick with a job until it's done? Without the Spirit giving me discernment, I'll get in the way of what God is trying to teach her from day to day.

Life is too short to live for only our own pleasure. C. S. Lewis expressed it perfectly when he said, "If we consider the unblushing promises of reward and the staggering nature of the rewards promised in the Gospels, it would seem that Our Lord finds our desires not too strong, but too weak. We are half-hearted creatures, fooling about with drink and sex and ambition when infinite joy is offered us, like an ignorant child who wants to go on making mud pies in a slum because he cannot imagine what is meant by the offer of a holiday at the sea. We are far too easily pleased."[3]

May we find our greatest pleasure in God so that all else pales by comparison. I pray that my daughter sees this kind of heart in me and discovers a life fully satisfied in him.

– 19 –

When She's Grieving

The LORD is close to the brokenhearted and saves those who are crushed in spirit.

Psalm 34:18

Brothers and sisters, we do not want you to be uninformed about those who sleep in death, so that you do not grieve like the rest of mankind, who have no hope. For we believe that Jesus died and rose again, and so we believe that God will bring with Jesus those who have fallen asleep in him.

1 Thessalonians 4:13–14

Praise be to the God and Father of our Lord Jesus Christ, the Father of compassion and the God of all comfort, who comforts us in all our troubles, so that we can comfort those in any trouble with the comfort we ourselves receive from God. For just as we share abundantly in the sufferings of Christ, so also our comfort abounds through Christ.

2 Corinthians 1:3–5

Father,

You know my daughter's pain. You know the loss she has suffered. In a life of relative comfort and peace, this kind of grief is unfamiliar and traumatic for her.

It's hard for me as her dad because I can't take the pain away. I can't fix what's broken or bring back what has been lost. I hurt for her and feel so weak and powerless.

I praise you for being what I cannot be. Thank you for your promise to remain close to her. We have the love of Christ, who can identify with our pain because of what he suffered on the cross. The comfort you bring is perfect and complete compared to what small gestures I could give.

Reveal yourself as Comforter to my daughter. Don't let her perception of you be clouded by her emotions. Speak into her heart and mind so she can see how real you are. Use this time of trouble to deepen her faith in your love.

Give me the courage to meet her in the pain. Let me be a listening ear and not try to "fix it" or make light of how she feels. Make me gentle and approachable so she can share her hurts and not walk through this alone. Teach me what true encouragement is—to point her to your goodness and truth.

Thank you for loving my daughter and giving us your hope. Amen.

– 20 –

When She Needs to Stay Pure

Flee from sexual immorality. All other sins a person commits are outside the body, but whoever sins sexually sins against their own body. Do you not know that your bodies are temples of the Holy Spirit, who is in you, whom you have received from God? You are not your own; you were bought at a price. Therefore honor God with your bodies.

1 Corinthians 6:18–20

For the grace of God has appeared that offers salvation to all people. It teaches us to say "No" to ungodliness and worldly passions, and to live self-controlled, upright and godly lives in this present age, while we wait for the blessed hope—the appearing of the glory of our great God and Savior, Jesus Christ, who gave himself for us to redeem us from all wickedness and to purify for himself a people that are his very own, eager to do what is good.

Titus 2:11–14

Lord God,

Your desire for my daughter is that she stay sexually pure and remain undefiled. You want her to remain set apart for her husband until her wedding day. In this world where promiscuity is the norm, your standard of purity is seen as unrealistic and ridiculous.

My daughter will hear that she should live to make herself happy. That she should please her boyfriend instead of her dad and her Lord. That she should look sexy rather than feminine and lovely. That if she holds on to her purity she's narrow-minded, rigid, self-righteous, or a fool.

Protect my daughter from believing those lies. Give her the wisdom to see that godliness and purity bring blessings that the world can only dream of. Help her to find complete satisfaction in living for you. Give her the courage to stand by your truth even if it brings misunderstanding and ridicule her way. Let her be convinced that the boundaries you set for us are an act of your love.

Give me wisdom as her father to protect her from those who would steal her innocence. May she feel such devotion and affirmation from me that the attentions of others would pale by comparison. Help her to understand all the good things her future marriage can hold if she cherishes her purity and guards her heart for her husband.

Thank you for creating my daughter and making her body a temple of your Spirit. May she trust in your promises to give her joy and a future with you if she surrenders her life to you today. Amen.

− 21 −

When She Needs to Honor Her Parents

Children, obey your parents in the Lord, for this is right. "Honor your father and mother"—which is the first commandment with a promise—"so that it may go well with you and that you may enjoy long life on the earth."

Ephesians 6:1–3

But mark this: There will be terrible times in the last days. People will be lovers of themselves, lovers of money, boastful, proud, abusive, disobedient to their parents, ungrateful, unholy, without love, unforgiving, slanderous, without self-control, brutal, not lovers of the good, treacherous, rash, conceited, lovers of pleasure rather than lovers of God—having a form of godliness but denying its power. Have nothing to do with such people.

2 Timothy 3:1–5

Father,

When I sit down to watch TV with my daughter, I see ridiculous parents and children who run their own lives. I hear sarcasm and disrespect of adults, and fathers who dishonor themselves by their childish behavior.

When my daughter visits her friends' homes, she often sees passive dads who have "checked out" of parenting through their own busyness or insecurity. Their kids have amazing privileges but virtually no responsibility. Parents are used for their money and transportation but not for guidance or relationship.

Place a covering over our home! Give me the courage to lead and teach my daughter. Give me the kind of integrity and strength that earn her respect. May I set an example of humility, self-control, and godliness that hold up a right standard for my daughter to live by. May I honor her mother by my words and actions, and may I encourage my daughter to do the same.

Protect my daughter from the influence of the world. Keep her mind from the lie that she's accountable to no one but herself. Help her to find security and peace living under the authority of you and her parents. Keep her conscience sensitive to when she's falling into any kind of rebellion, even if it's just in her thoughts or attitudes.

Thank you for giving my daughter the promise of peace that obedience brings. Thank you for delivering us from the hopelessness of the world. Keep us near to you. Amen.

– 22 –

When She Must Submit to Authority

Let everyone be subject to the governing authorities, for there is no authority except that which God has established. The authorities that exist have been established by God. Consequently, whoever rebels against the authority is rebelling against what God has instituted, and those who do so will bring judgment on themselves. For rulers hold no terror for those who do right, but for those who do wrong. Do you want to be free from fear of the one in authority? Then do what is right and you will be commended.

Romans 13:1–3

Have confidence in your leaders and submit to their authority, because they keep watch over you as those who must give an account. Do this so that their work will be a joy, not a burden, for that would be of no benefit to you.

Hebrews 13:17

Almighty God,

Thank you for raising up a government to establish protection and order in our land. We are fully aware of the weaknesses of our leaders, but we know that without any authority in place we would live in utter chaos.

Give my daughter a respectful, obedient heart toward the authorities in her life. May she submit herself to the wisdom of her pastor, the requirements of her school, and the laws of our city and country. Bring protection and blessing to her through those you have placed in leadership over her.

I know that obedience will bring her peace and a good reputation. Whether it's good grades, safety, a clean conscience, or personal freedom, may she experience the benefits of honoring her leaders. May she take hold of the wisdom in your Word that counsels her to obey.

Keep me from being a stumbling block by my own attitudes about authority. Keep me from going out of bounds in my driving, my finances, and the way I express my opinions about our government. Make me respectful of the management at work. Guard my words from criticizing our pastor and elders. Don't allow me to use my personal freedoms to slander anyone or foster a poor attitude in my daughter.

Thank you for your great love that provides protection for us through our government. Thank you for the leadership in our lives that directs us in the right way to go. Let us look to you as our ultimate authority—give us hearts that delight to do your will. May your wonderful name be glorified through our respect and submission. Amen.

– 23 –

When She's Making Plans

Trust in the Lord with all your heart and lean not on your own understanding; in all your ways submit to him, and he will make your paths straight.

Proverbs 3:5–6

Therefore, I urge you, brothers and sisters, in view of God's mercy, to offer your bodies as a living sacrifice, holy and pleasing to God—this is your true and proper worship. Do not conform to the pattern of this world, but be transformed by the renewing of your mind. Then you will be able to test and approve what God's will is—his good, pleasing and perfect will.

Romans 12:1–2

LORD, *I know that people's lives are not their own; it is not for them to direct their steps.*

Jeremiah 10:23

Father,

In the movies and fairy tales my daughter has seen, the characters seek to "follow their heart" and "create their own destiny." When the characters finally get everything they desire, it's called living happily ever after.

Lord, I know that we can never find joy outside of your will! Whenever I've gone my own way or charted my own course, it's only brought frustration and disappointment. Nothing can equal the peace that obedience brings.

Help my daughter to see that sometimes your plans include giving up her own goals and preferences. When she leans on her own understanding, she assumes every difficulty is a mistake rather than something you're using to bring her right where you want her to be. Grow her faith so she can trust you with her future. Help her to surrender her life to your control.

Transform our thinking so we have the mind of Christ rather than the world. Give us *your* priorities, instead of us just pursuing our own personal gain. May we surrender our hearts fully to you and offer our bodies as "living sacrifices." Keep us from living for ourselves, setting our own agendas, and placing our desires above yours.

Thank you for the plans you have for my daughter. I know your will for her is "good, pleasing, and perfect." Help her to embrace those plans and discover how incredible her life will be if she lives it completely for you. Amen.

– 24 –

When She Hears False Teaching

But I am afraid that just as Eve was deceived by the serpent's cunning, your minds may somehow be led astray from your sincere and pure devotion to Christ.

2 Corinthians 11:3

Watch out for false prophets. They come to you in sheep's cloth-ing, but inwardly they are ferocious wolves. By their fruit you will recognize them. Do people pick grapes from thornbushes, or figs from thistles? Likewise every good tree bears good fruit, but a bad tree bears bad fruit.

Matthew 7:15–17

So then, just as you received Christ Jesus as Lord, continue to live your lives in him, rooted and built up in him, strengthened in the faith as you were taught, and overflowing with thankful-ness. See to it that no one takes you captive through hollow and deceptive philosophy, which depends on human tradition and the elemental spiritual forces of this world rather than on Christ.

Colossians 2:6–8

Lord God,

So many voices speak to my daughter's mind. I can't con-trol if her teachers will acknowledge you as Creator. If our politicians will protect the lives of the unborn. If her friends believe that the Bible has any authority. If her relatives respect our family's standards for right and wrong. People near and dear to my daughter may bring confusing messages from their own lack of understanding. As her dad, it's tempting to try to hide her from the world so I can filter every idea that she might be exposed to.

However, what my daughter needs even more than my protection is discernment. When the world says that money and fame are the ultimate goals, keep her focused on living for you. When they say everyone can create their own moral code, give her devotion to your holy ways. When they say that she can please you through traditions or rituals, remind her that you desire the love of her heart.

Give my daughter eyes to see the "wolves" that would tear her faith apart. By your Spirit, help her recognize good and bad fruit in others so she knows whom to trust. Put a guard over our relationship so I can maintain influence in her life. Make me strong in the knowledge of your Word so I can share your truth wisely and accurately.

She needs her faith to be built up in you—bring godly men and women into her life who instruct her well. Strengthen her faith and put down deep roots of truth in her heart. Sustain her so she can live continually in you, free from captivity to any deception. You are her hope and shield. Amen.

– 25 –

When She Needs Good Advice

The way of a fool is right in his own eyes, but a wise man listens to advice.

Proverbs 12:15 ESV

Listen, my sons, to a father's instruction; pay attention and gain understanding. . . . Listen, my son, accept what I say, and the years of your life will be many. I instruct you in the way of wisdom and lead you along straight paths. When you walk, your steps will not be hampered; when you run, you will not stumble. Hold on to instruction, do not let it go; guard it well, for it is your life.

Lord,

I thank you for offering us the opportunity to find wisdom and learning. You don't abandon us to ignorance. However, sometimes in our own laziness or pride we are happy to stay as we are. We swallow the opinions of the world around us without question. We leave books to gather dust on the shelf. We avoid hearing teaching at church that might stretch or challenge us. We hang out with friends who accept us just as we are rather than encouraging us to grow in wisdom and turn away from sin.

Protect my daughter from a stubborn heart that rejects the advice of her parents. Place caring people in her life who have the courage to speak the truth and point her to you. Open her ears to hear and understand your Word, and create sensitivity to your Spirit's leading and guidance. Open doors of learning for her—quality books, gifted teachers, new experiences and challenges—that will renew her mind and make her more like Jesus.

Make me a wise father, able to give advice and wisdom to my daughter. Give me the right words to speak at just the right times. Keep my daughter on a straight path as she walks through this life. Let her see the great value of the instruction she's been given. Allow her to have an unshakeable understanding of right and wrong. Protect her from making destructive choices that bring pain and heartache into her life.

Thank you again for the gifts of knowledge and wisdom. May we be faithful to listen and allow you to change us from the inside out. Amen.

A Dad's Story

When my daughter Sara was six years old, she was standing on a chair, helping her mother cook some macaroni and cheese, and while she was reaching for something, the chair tipped over. In the process of trying to catch herself, she dumped the boiling hot water over her face, chest, and arm. Over the next few hours, most of the burned skin came off. While we were in the burn center, the doctors felt the need to "scrub" off the skin that hadn't come off on its own. Needless to say, this is a very painful process and a horrible thing for parents to have to watch. After the first two times they did this, we were totally at our wits' end and didn't know how we could allow them to do it the third and final time that they insisted was necessary. They informed us that this time would probably be worse than the first two times because of the extent of the scrubbing they would need to do. They also informed us that they couldn't give her enough morphine to kill the pain as it would be too dangerous.

I told my wife, Emily, to wait out in the hall and text everyone she could think of, asking them to pray for a miracle. They brought in a few extra nurses to help hold Sara down while they did the procedure. By this time she had come to dread seeing doctors and nurses coming her way, and so she was very upset when she saw them approaching her. As I stood there holding her hand and praying, she calmed right down—and the nurses and I watched in amazement as the doctor completed the procedure with Sara lying there calmly taking it all in. The only explanation I need for this is that God heard the desperate prayers of his children and chose to step in and perform a miracle.

Phil Mast, North Virginia

– 26 –

When She Needs to Give

Command them to do good, to be rich in good deeds, and to be generous and willing to share. In this way they will lay up treasure for themselves as a firm foundation for the coming age, so that they may take hold of the life that is truly life.

1 Timothy 6:18–19

The point is this: whoever sows sparingly will also reap sparingly, and whoever sows bountifully will also reap bountifully. Each one must give as he has decided in his heart, not reluctantly or under compulsion, for God loves a cheerful giver. And God is able to make all grace abound to you, so that having all sufficiency in all things at all times, you may abound in every good work. As it is written, "He has distributed freely, he has given to the poor; his righteousness endures forever."

2 Corinthians 9:6–9 ESV

Father,

You have been so generous to me! I have a home, talents and abilities, people who care about me, and a beautiful child who is the treasure of my heart. You have poured out your blessings on my daughter as well. She has friends and family, material things, opportunities to learn and explore, and the energy and promise of her youth.

Keep us from selfish hearts that hoard the wonderful blessings you've given. It's easy to forget that you are the source of all we have and become proud and give ourselves the credit. It is tempting to keep wanting more and more, focusing on what we don't have rather than on how incredibly blessed we are.

Fill us with compassion for those who struggle. If my daughter is rich in friends, let her reach out to girls who are lonely. If she has a closet full of attractive outfits, give her a tender heart for girls who can't afford the clothing they need. When she has more than she can eat, help her to remember those who go hungry. When she is warm and comfortable in her bedroom, may she have compassion for the homeless and a heart for hospitality.

Show us real, practical ways we can share with others. Lead us to ministries we can partner to help those who are struggling. Keep us from accumulating more and more, and challenge us to give what we have. Protect us from loving our money—give us a cheerful spirit about giving to anyone in need! May we be faithful to care for our family and the body of Christ, not just with our finances but with our time and energy too.

Thank you for sending Jesus as a perfect example of giving and serving. Transform us and make us like him. Amen.

– 27 –

When She Needs to Work

Whatever you do, work at it with all your heart, as working for the Lord, not for human masters, since you know that you will receive an inheritance from the Lord as a reward. It is the Lord Christ you are serving.

Colossians 3:23–24

A lazy person craves food and there is none, but the appetite of hard-working people is satisfied.

Proverbs 13:4 GW

Lord God,

It is so easy for my daughter to sit back and let life carry on without her. She can lose herself in surfing the internet, watching TV, sleeping, shopping, or playing video games. She can wake up in the morning and expect the day to be about her own gratification. If demands are placed on her time and energy, she feels resentful. Work is just something to put up with as a means of paying for her own pleasure.

It's easy to forget that "we are God's handiwork, created in Christ Jesus to do good works, which God prepared in advance for us to do" (Eph. 2:10). Stir up my daughter's heart to work, and to work diligently. Give her a sense of purpose for what is before her each day.

Give my daughter motivation to tackle her studies and chores. Sometimes she wants to quit before she's done or she's satisfied with bare-minimum effort. She will do as little as she has to, to keep her parents or teachers "off her back." She'll be tempted to pursue excellence only in things that bring her attention or praise. Teach her the satisfaction that comes from doing an excellent job. Help her to enjoy a challenge and to be energized by new projects. Give her a reputation for being faithful and responsible. Reveal the blessings you have in store when she works in obedience to you.

Keep us from working hard simply for our own gain. May we work "as for the Lord" instead of just trying to impress other people. May we be just as diligent when we're alone as we are when others are watching. When others around us accomplish something with excellence, let us cheer them on and celebrate the results. Let us praise you for giving us the strength and ability to create, to build, and to learn.

We want to serve you with all of our strength. Train our hearts to value work and to obey you in all things. Allow us to experience your inheritance and reward. Amen.

Her Identity

In a recent interview I read with pastor and bestselling author Mark Driscoll, he comments on the topic of identity as it relates to his daughter:

> Our oldest daughter is 15. When it comes to identity, the pressure is immense on everyone in general, but especially for young women—from how much you weigh, to the friends you have, your grade point average, the music you like, the hobbies you enjoy, the sports you play, the clothes you wear, and the technology you own. All are identifying markers of who you are. On social media we create an identity only to have it scrutinized. Much of parental work, then, is knowing who we are in Christ and then helping our children understand who they are in Christ. In that sense, parenting is discipling.[4]

My greatest hope as a dad is for my daughter to find her identity in God and God alone! I want her to see herself the way he does rather than how she sees herself when she looks in the mirror or compares herself to others. Everywhere my daughter turns she's told who she should be—intelligent, beautiful, talented, funny, popular—and it has nothing to do with being a child of God.

My prayer is for my daughter to abandon herself completely to God, because it is the only way she will ever find true peace, joy, and acceptance. Everything around her is going to try and pull her away from the truth and tell her she's missing out on something in life. I have to pray for her to stand strong to resist the temptation to find her identity in the pattern of this world. And I have to ask God for wisdom and boldness to speak into her life, pointing my daughter to her true source of worth and acceptance.

The Lord will hear my prayers when I ask for guidance in talking about my daughter's identity. He will reveal to me what kinds of qualities I've been validating in her. Does she only hear affirmation for her appearance and performance? Or does she hear me praising her for showing kindness? Waiting patiently even when she's excited? Obeying the first time instead of arguing? Having a grateful attitude instead of complaining? Celebrating the blessings of others instead of just thinking of herself? If she sees me valuing the character of her heart instead of just her external achievements, she'll have a better picture of what matters to God.

If my daughter attempts to find her identity in the wrong places she'll end up with heartache and pain. She'll never be able to reach the standard she has set in her mind so she'll always feel like a failure, and she will be left open to the dangers of eating disorders, unhealthy dating relationships, addictions, and compromising her values to please others. If she doesn't know who she truly is, she'll look to other people to define her. She'll become caught up in living for others instead of the God who loves her the most.

I pray for wisdom as a dad to know the boundaries to set to guard my daughter's mind. It takes courage to be the "bad guy" when I have to say no to music, movies, and magazines that pressure my daughter to look and act a certain way. I may have to put away the checkbook and delay my daughter's gratification for that possession she thinks she has to have to be happy. Yet through all of this I need to stay compassionate and understanding—she's in a battle and I'm here to help, not make her feel guilty for struggling.

I had a conversation with my teenager recently, and she told me that if you get labeled as a certain kind of person in middle school, that image sticks all the way through high school. No matter how you might grow or change, she said, "that becomes who you are." Girls feel incredible pressure to establish their identity in the eyes of others before they've even had a chance to discover who they are for themselves. I'm thankful that my daughter is loved by God and can find freedom from this worry. I pray she will find rest and security by embracing who he declares her to be—an heir of promise, holy and beloved, a friend of God, a new creation, and a chosen one.

As fathers, we need to be careful to let our daughters be themselves. If you're quiet and reserved but your daughter is a lively extrovert who wears her emotions on her sleeve, ask God for help to enjoy those unique qualities. If you were a straight-A student and have pursued an intellectually demanding career, pray for patience if she's not the scholar you'd like her to be. If she'd rather practice her violin in her room while you'd like to see her running on the soccer field, praise God for her talents instead of trying to push her into a different activity. Realize that your daughter is sensitive and can pick up on your disapproval. If she thinks she's disappointing you with her personality and interests, it will shake her confidence in God's acceptance of her as well.

If our girls become able to see themselves as children of God, created and loved by the Lord of all, they will be free to do amazing things in this life. They can escape the trap of living to please others and live for him instead. They will discover his good, perfect, and pleasing will for their lives and the good works God has prepared in advance for them to do (Rom. 12:2; Eph. 2:10). And we fathers will have the amazing privilege of watching them grow in joy and grace right before our eyes.

– 28 –

When She Needs Self-Control

Like a city whose walls are broken through is a person who lacks self-control.

Proverbs 25:28

For the grace of God has appeared that offers salvation to all people. It teaches us to say "No" to ungodliness and worldly passions, and to live self-controlled, upright and godly lives in this present age, while we wait for the blessed hope—the appearing of the glory of our great God and Savior, Jesus Christ, who gave himself for us to redeem us from all wickedness and to purify for himself a people that are his very own, eager to do what is good.

Titus 2:11–14

Lord,

It seems like part of childhood to be impulsive. Walking in the rain can become a full-blown mud bath in no time! A little dispute over a toy can quickly become a screaming match. Snacking on a couple of cookies can lead to the jar being emptied in one sitting. My daughter's efforts to clean her room can fall to the side when she gets distracted by a book found under the bed. Checking her phone for a moment can become an hour-long texting session.

Part of my daughter's maturity means growing in self-control. I pray you would give her your grace to slow down and think before she speaks. To have a healthy appetite that says no when she's full. To "look before she leaps" when she's having a fun, rowdy time that could go too far. To take a deep breath before she reacts in anger. To remember her curfew instead of losing track of the time. To be diligent and focused when she has a task to accomplish.

Use me as an example of godliness in these matters. Keep me from giving way to too much of anything, whether it's sports, work, entertainment, or emotions that become out of balance in my life. Rein me in when I'm heading out-of-bounds so my daughter can see what self-control should look like.

I thank you that in love you want to bring us into a close relationship with you. You know that becoming mastered by our emotions and impulses will only keep us from the wonderful life you desire. Guide us by your Spirit as we live in you. Amen.

When She's Looking for Fun

Rob and Joanna Teigen

For you were once darkness, but now you are light in the Lord.
Live as children of light (for the fruit of the light consists in all
goodness, righteousness and truth) and find out what pleases the
Lord. Have nothing to do with the fruitless deeds of darkness,
but rather expose them. It is shameful even to mention what the
disobedient do in secret.

Ephesians 5:8–12

I will be careful to lead a blameless life—when will you come to
me? I will conduct the affairs of my house with a blameless heart.
I will not look with approval on anything that is vile. I hate what
faithless people do; I will have no part in it. The perverse of heart
shall be far from me; I will have nothing to do with what is evil.

Psalm 101:2–4

Father,

The number of forms of entertainment is growing every day. My daughter and I can access all kinds of music, games, and videos on our TV, computers, tablets, and phones. We could never exhaust the list of apps available to download, with more and more created all the time.

While rest and relaxation are gifts for our good, my daughter can find herself making entertainment the focal point of her day. She needs your wisdom to know when to put aside distractions. She needs self-control to be able to turn off her devices when she's wasting time trying to beat just one more level!

Most of the time, the shows we watch and the games we play are fun and harmless. But I know that we can become desensitized to material that is dishonoring to you through constant exposure that makes violence and overt sexuality seem commonplace. We can find ourselves laughing at behaviors that you consider shameful. Even during a family-friendly program, advertisers flood our eyes with images that steal my daughter's innocence.

Guard my daughter's eyes, heart, and mind from anything that makes sin seem trivial. Keep her thoughts centered on admirable, pure, and excellent things that please you. Give her an inner sense of right and wrong that is offended by perversity and darkness.

Sometimes living by your standards can be tough. My daughter may have to stand out from her friends by making different choices. She may experience frustration when I put limits on her computer activity that she's not mature enough to understand. Strengthen us by your Spirit so we can follow your leading, and keep us unified as we make decisions about our entertainment.

Thank you for setting us free from the darkness and giving us life. You are perfect and full of goodness and truth—may we love you fully and live in your light. Amen.

– 30 –

When She's Choosing Her Words

Do not let any unwholesome talk come out of your mouths, but only what is helpful for building others up according to their needs, that it may benefit those who listen.

Ephesians 4:29

A good man brings good things out of the good stored up in his heart, and an evil man brings evil things out of the evil stored up in his heart. For the mouth speaks what the heart is full of.

Luke 6:45

Those who guard their lips preserve their lives, but those who speak rashly will come to ruin.

Proverbs 13:3

Lord God,

Our ears are flooded every day with sarcasm, profanity, flippant remarks, inappropriate humor, and complaining words. This "unwholesome talk" can saturate our minds and influence the way we express ourselves. And, Lord, you know that "we all stumble in many ways. Anyone who is never at fault in what they say is perfect, able to keep their whole body in check" (James 3:2). We are so far from perfect, and our battle to "tame the tongue" never ends.

I pray for my daughter, that she will speak words of goodness and honesty. Use her as a blessing to her classmates and family by the way she encourages others. May her kind, honoring speech reflect Jesus in her life and increase her testimony of you.

Keep her from mindless chatter and joking words that tear others down. Give her the self-control to filter her speech before she lets foolish words fly out without thinking. She can bring so much trouble on herself—a ruined reputation, broken relationships, and missed opportunities—by giving way to impulsive words.

Give her the ability to be still and listen. May she have discernment about whom she lets speak into her life. Fill her with courage to walk away from friends or entertainers whose words drag her down or pull her away from you. May your Word be written on her heart to guide her as she grows.

Use my words to bless my daughter. Keep me from harsh criticism, sarcasm, or thoughtless put-downs that will crush her spirit. May I set an example of integrity and grace in how I speak to her and others. Fill my mouth with your truth in every situation by the power of your Spirit. Amen.

– 31 –

When She's Preparing for Marriage

Do not be yoked together with unbelievers. For what do righteousness and wickedness have in common? Or what fellowship can light have with darkness? What harmony is there between Christ and Belial? What does a believer have in common with an unbeliever?

2 Corinthians 6:14–15

Husbands, love your wives, just as Christ loved the church and gave himself up for her.

Ephesians 5:25

Husbands, in the same way be considerate as you live with your wives, and treat them with respect as the weaker partner and as heirs with you of the gracious gift of life, so that nothing will hinder your prayers. Finally, all of you, be like-minded, be sympathetic, love one another, be compassionate and humble.

1 Peter 3:7–8

Father,

Although my daughter is young, I know that the years pass so quickly. Before I know it she'll be wearing a beautiful white dress and placing her hand in mine to walk down the aisle.

I pray today for the man my daughter will marry. You created him, love him, and are already shaping him into the husband he will be someday. Keep his body safe from illness and injury, defend his mind against ignorance and false teaching, and protect his emotions by surrounding him with faithful love and care.

May my daughter's husband be a wholehearted follower of you. May he commit his path to your authority. Fill him with your Spirit that he may live in purity and the knowledge of

God. May he love your Word and have it hidden in his heart that he might not sin against you (Ps. 119:11).

Strengthen him to lead his family well. Give him honor among his peers and a blameless reputation. Reveal his spiritual gifts and give him a passion to serve the body of Christ. Give him the wisdom to make excellent decisions and escape temptation.

Even now, create a compassionate spirit in him so he will cherish my daughter. Give him the humility to serve her well and resolve any conflicts that arise. Motivate him to provide for her, protect her heart, and sacrifice for her well-being. May the love he shows my daughter be a reflection of the amazing way you love your people.

Protect their marriage—keep them from holding grudges that eat away at the unity you desire for them. Give them faithfulness so no other affection can come between them. Let them lay down their own selfish desires so they can be a blessing to each other. May they find joy in their life together as they follow you in everything. Amen.

– 32 –

When She's Doubting God

Yet he did not waver through unbelief regarding the promise of God, but was strengthened in his faith and gave glory to God, being fully persuaded that God had power to do what he had promised.

Romans 4:20–21

I pray that out of his glorious riches he may strengthen you with power through his Spirit in your inner being, so that Christ may dwell in your hearts through faith. And I pray that you, being

*rooted and established in love, may have power, together with
all the Lord's holy people, to grasp how wide and long and high
and deep is the love of Christ, and to know this love that sur-
passes knowledge—that you may be filled to the measure of all
the fullness of God.*

Ephesians 3:16–19

Lord God,

Our greatest struggle is to hold on to faith in you. You are
faithful and never change, but we lose our confidence in you
so easily. When my daughter struggles or sees the evil in the
world around her, she isn't sure of your power or goodness.
She can feel that your promises in Scripture are answered for
others and not for her. Jesus returned to heaven so long ago,
and she wonders if he's ever really coming back for us.

Where are you when natural disasters kill and destroy? When
evil men abandon or murder innocent children? When good
people lose everything but selfish schemers get whatever they
want? When the "greats" in our society dismiss your Word
as a fairy tale? We need your help to see you clearly when the
world is such a broken place.

My daughter is young, and the testing of her faith is new
and scary for her. She's not sure how to reconcile the good God
she's been taught about with the bad situation she's confronted
with. I pray by your Spirit you would give her strength. Give
her an unshakeable belief in your love. Let her faith rise above
her emotions and questions so it can overshadow all her fears
and doubts.

Draw your people around my daughter to lift her up and
encourage her. Use my faith and worship, weak as they are,
to demonstrate your love. Write your Word on her heart so its
truth permeates her life.

Give my daughter power to grasp the limitless love of Christ.
And in this, fill her with your fullness. In your fullness we see
life-changing power unleashed in our lives. We see promises
fulfilled. We see the body of Christ joined together. We are

lifted beyond what our eyes can see to experience the love of
heaven itself. Amen.

– 33 –

When She Needs Healing

Do you not know? Have you not heard? The LORD *is the everlasting God, the Creator of the ends of the earth. He will not grow
tired or weary, and his understanding no one can fathom. He
gives strength to the weary and increases the power of the weak.
Even youths grow tired and weary, and young men stumble and
fall; but those who hope in the* LORD *will renew their strength.
They will soar on wings like eagles; they will run and not grow
weary, they will walk and not be faint.*

Isaiah 40:28–31

Praise the LORD, *my soul; all my inmost being, praise his holy
name. Praise the* LORD, *my soul, and forget not all his benefits—who forgives all your sins and heals all your diseases, who
redeems your life from the pit and crowns you with love and
compassion, who satisfies your desires with good things so that
your youth is renewed like the eagle's.*

Psalm 103:1–5

Loving Father,

You are the Lord not just of our hearts and minds, but of
our bodies as well. We were created by you and are "fearfully
and wonderfully made" (Ps. 139:14). But in this imperfect world
we experience illness and fatigue. Our bodies age and become
fragile. Stress and overwork can beat us down until we become
sick and are forced to take a break.

You know our weaknesses. You have compassion on my
daughter because even though she's young, she's not invincible.

Health issues interfere with her daily life. She catches the virus going around at school. The big game leaves her bruised and sore. An accident keeps her on the sidelines for weeks. The stress and strain of a hectic schedule wear her out and discourage her spirit.

Lord, lift her up. As her Great Physician, bring healing to her body. Breathe energy and life into her when she just can't go another step. Give my daughter your hope in times of illness or fatigue. Use those experiences to teach her that you are her strength. Give her the wisdom to pursue fitness, nutrition, and adequate rest, but may she understand that her power is truly found in you.

Give me wisdom to know how to care for her. If she needs to lighten her load, help me to set wise limits on her schedule. If she needs more rest or nutrition, help me to provide. If she needs encouragement to hang in there and keep going, give me words to speak that will build her up.

Be the healer of my daughter's soul as well. In your mercy, may she find forgiveness and comfort in you. When she stumbles and falls, set her back on her feet that she may continue walking with you. When she is confused or deceived, renew her mind with your truth.

You are our Great Physician. You heal our wounds and satisfy every desire of our hearts. We are overwhelmed with your love. Amen.

– 34 –

When She Needs to Confess

If we claim to be without sin, we deceive ourselves and the truth is not in us. If we confess our sins, he is faithful and just and will forgive us our sins and purify us from all unrighteousness.

1 John 1:8–9

Blessed is the one whose transgressions are forgiven, whose sins are covered. Blessed is the one whose sin the LORD does not count against them and in whose spirit is no deceit. When I kept silent, my bones wasted away through my groaning all day long. For day and night your hand was heavy on me; my strength was sapped as in the heat of summer. Then I acknowledged my sin to you and did not cover up my iniquity. I said, "I will confess my transgressions to the LORD." And you forgave the guilt of my sin.

Psalm 32:1–5

Almighty God,

In this modern age we don't hear the word *sin* very often. We talk about our mistakes, our poor choices, and our oversights. We aim for good behavior rather than holiness. We compare our actions to the world around us (and feel rather good about ourselves) rather than living by your perfect standards.

Give my daughter the humility to see where she falls short of your glory. Enable her to name her sins for what they are and not pass them off as mere weaknesses. Use the Spirit's conviction in her heart to reveal her need for your forgiveness.

I pray that my daughter would not be satisfied with just being a "good girl." Teach her to love your ways and the life of holiness she is called to. Let her run to you when she falls, that she may experience the peace and blessings of a purified heart.

If my daughter is holding on to a sinful habit right now, help her to see how it is separating her from you. Give her the wisdom to see that continuing in sin will only bring pain and destruction into her life. Show her what she has to lose if she chooses to go her own way.

Thank you for your love that never says no when we seek you. That restores our strength and hope when we confess our sins to you. That never gives up on us even when we've given up on ourselves. You make us new and set us free. Amen.

– 35 –

When She Struggles with Gossip

A perverse person stirs up conflict, and a gossip separates close friends.

Proverbs 16:28

Whoever goes around as a gossip tells secrets. Do not associate with a person whose mouth is always open.

Proverbs 20:19 GW

Live such good lives among the pagans that, though they accuse you of doing wrong, they may see your good deeds and glorify God on the day he visits us.

1 Peter 2:12

Remind the people to be subject to rulers and authorities, to be obedient, to be ready to do whatever is good, to slander no one, to be peaceable and considerate, and always to be gentle toward everyone.

Titus 3:1–2

Lord,

My daughter is wounded today by the gossip being spread about her. She feels betrayed and misunderstood. She doesn't know how to restore her reputation. She doesn't know whom she can trust.

I place my daughter and this situation in your hands. Bring the truth into the light so that the rumors completely dissolve. Fill her true friends with compassion and the courage to stand by her no matter what others say. Bring unity and peace to all who are involved. Restore relationships that have been strained or broken.

It is tempting for my daughter to retaliate by spreading gossip herself. Keep her from slandering anyone when she's upset or angry. Keep her calm and peaceful in the knowledge that you are working things together for her good. Give her the humility to admit any mistakes on her part that could have contributed to the issue in the first place.

Rein me in, Lord. It's tempting as her dad to want to get in the middle of the situation and "fix it." Help me to trust you for the outcome, and give me the wisdom to know when to speak and when to be still.

I pray that this experience will teach my daughter compassion. Help her to forgive those who let her down. Make her more sensitive to her own speech in the future, since she knows the pain a careless word can bring. Use her as a peacemaker and an example of your kindness.

Thank you for your faithful love that shows us the way. Amen.

A Dad's Story

Our oldest daughter was just starting kindergarten, and like most parents would be, my wife and I were concerned about what school our child would attend and which teacher to request. We listed out the pros and cons, nitpicking through what we thought was best for our daughter. When it came to requesting a particular kindergarten teacher, our daughter took a different approach. We asked her opinion about which teacher she would like to request after an open house at the school, and we shared our pros and cons with her. She responded matter-of-factly, "Oh, don't worry. I told God that he could pick!" Now, we have taught our daughter to pray about decisions, but this seemed a little odd. There were plenty of reasons why we thought one teacher would be the right choice by far. However, our daughter was insistent that "God knows best," and we decided that this could be a life lesson. We ended up not requesting a particular teacher and prayed with her for God's choice. Our daughter started the first day of school, and when we picked her up from school that day, she wasn't so sure she liked her teacher much. But two weeks later, and continuing throughout the year, our daughter came home from school telling stories about how her teacher was "perfect" for her. We gathered that the teacher was structured, with low tolerance for chaos in the class, and yet gentle in instruction and discipline. Those are character qualities that cannot be observed in a quick open-house experience. Only God could have known which teacher would be right for our daughter, and he graciously provided an answer to our prayer. We never forgot that lesson and often still use it to remember that God knows the future and we can trust him when making decisions about "tomorrow."

Joel Shank, children's ministry pastor, Grand Rapids, Michigan

– 36 –

When She's Facing a Change

Jesus Christ is the same yesterday and today and forever.
Hebrews 13:8

There is a time for everything, and a season for every activity under the heavens: a time to be born and a time to die, a time to plant and a time to uproot, a time to kill and a time to heal, a time to tear down and a time to build, a time to weep and a time to laugh, a time to mourn and a time to dance, a time to scatter stones and a time to gather them, a time to embrace and a time to refrain from embracing, a time to search and a time to give

*up, a time to keep and a time to throw away, a time to tear and
a time to mend, a time to be silent and a time to speak, a time
to love and a time to hate, a time for war and a time for peace.*

Ecclesiastes 3:1–8

*The steadfast love of the L*ord *never ceases; his mercies never
come to an end; they are new every morning; great is your
faithfulness.*

Lamentations 3:22–23 ESV

Father,

We find a sense of security when our days are predictable and
we think we know what to expect. We like order and routine,
the cycle of the days and seasons, and walking a straight path
toward our dreams and goals.

In your wisdom, you remind us that everything has a season.
We never know when we'll enter a period of loss and have to
give up someone or something we cherish. So many things can
change unexpectedly: our address, our career path, our best
friend, our health, our safety, and even our life in this world.

Help my daughter to accept the changes that come her way.
Let her find security and peace in you instead of other people
or circumstances. May her heart's home be heaven rather than
our mailing address! May she find you to be her closest friend
instead of relying only on girls whose loyalty and kindness
can be so inconsistent.

Sometimes change means saying good-bye or giving up the
goal we were committed to. Give her wisdom to know when
to simplify her schedule, when to let go of a relationship that's
tearing her down, or when to surrender a hobby that's crowd-
ing out more meaningful activities.

Give her confidence to face new challenges and experiences—
let her embrace new classrooms and opportunities with ex-
citement. Fill her with courage to reach out and build new
friendships. Silence the critical voices that discourage her and
break her confidence.

Thank you for being our constant, unchanging God. No matter what we face from day to day, you are with us. We praise you for the peace and hope we find in you. Amen.

Her Purity

God did not call us to be impure, but to live a holy life.

1 Thessalonians 4:7

But among you there must not even be a hint of sexual immorality, or of any kind of impurity, or of greed, because these are improper for God's holy people.

Ephesians 5:3

It seems nearly impossible to convince young people that the reason God has told them to wait for sex until marriage is because he loves them! How do we persuade them that he's not trying to keep something amazing out of their hands when everything around us portrays sex as a natural part of love? Kids watch movies and TV shows and even listen to music that assumes sex is a part of every dating relationship. The attitude is that it's just another way to have fun, everyone's doing it, and it's no big deal. Our culture has stopped taking sex seriously. By offering the freedom to share intimacy with anyone and everyone, we've lost the awareness that through sex "the two will become one flesh" (1 Cor. 6:16).

But when you see all the ways casual sex has affected our society, individuals, and even ourselves, you can see why God set such a high standard for purity for his children that he loves. Young people suffer high rates of diseases, teen pregnancies, abortions, and emotional struggles because they don't understand the consequences of their actions.

Addiction to pornography by both men and women is at an all-time high and continues to grow, permanently distorting the beauty of intimacy in marriage. The average age for a child's first exposure to pornography is eleven years old, and 90 percent of kids ages eight to eighteen have viewed it online.[5] I'm not going to try and count how many adults and fathers are using porn on a daily basis. But I wonder how many dads *aren't* talking to their kids about purity because after their kids go to bed at night they're visiting websites and viewing magazines that have damaged their own sexual integrity.

I know committed men of God who battle with lust and pornography even though it goes against everything they believe in. Sexual sin has a unique ability to entrap us like no other temptation we face. To make it worse, graphic movies and pornography are more easily available now than ever. Such easy access creates a stumbling block at every turn for the man who is trying to keep his way pure.

Many of us have compromised our sexual purity in the past in ways we're not proud of. Dads can feel they're unqualified to hold their kids to God's standard since they failed in that area themselves when they were young. We're afraid of being hypocrites by asking our children to live out values that we didn't hold to ourselves. It's important to remember that in Christ, we are new creations. The man you are today does know the truth and seeks to live by it. Don't let the enemy keep you from challenging your daughter in this area because of something the Lord has already forgiven and removed "as far as the east is from the west" (Ps. 103:12).

I don't think it's wise to air our dirty laundry to our kids, but it can help them to know that everyone wrestles with sexual sin and temptation at some point. They'll be blessed by having a dad who's compassionate about what they're going through. The Lord even promises that he identifies with our struggle. He says, "We do not have a high priest who is unable to empathize with our weaknesses, but we have one who has been tempted in every way, just as we are—yet he did not sin. Let us then approach God's throne of grace with confidence, so that we may receive mercy and find grace to help us in our time of need"

(Heb. 4:15–16). Because of Christ our daughters don't have to go through it alone!

When it comes to praying for our daughter's purity, sometimes it's hard to know what to say, other than *Dear God, please kill any young man who tries to touch my daughter.* That's probably not the approach we should take! Perhaps we can ask that she stays so secure in the love of God and her dad that she doesn't need the affection of another guy to find her worth. And that she makes mindful choices along the way, not giving ground in small areas that will lead to giving up everything in the end. That she surrounds herself with friends and mentors who follow God, giving accountability when she's straying off the right path. We can pray for God to give us wisdom as parents to set boundaries around her social activities and entertainment choices that could influence her attitudes about modesty and sex. And we can pray that she trusts the Lord for her future—that he intends for her to have a beautiful, loving relationship with a man of God who will cherish her mind, body, and soul.

When we see so many kids falling away from the values they were raised with, we can wonder if praying for our daughters really does any good. We can think, *Maybe kids are just going to do what kids are going to do.* Don't give up hope that your influence and prayers make a difference! God reassures us in his Word that "this is the confidence we have in approaching God: that if we ask anything according to his will, he hears us. And if we know that he hears us—whatever we ask—we know that we have what we asked of him" (1 John 5:14–15). Ask God to develop your trust in him as you place your daughter in his hands.

For dads who are grieving because their daughter has already lost her purity and innocence in some way, take heart. God is in the business of making us new. He offers forgiveness, restoration, and a new beginning. Ask for his help in working through your anger and disappointment. Share Scriptures with your daughter about God's grace, such as 1 John 1:9, "If we confess our sins, he is faithful and just and will forgive us our sins and purify us from all unrighteousness." What an incredible promise to hold on to!

Our Father cherishes our daughters in every way, just as we do. In him we can find hope for our daughters' futures. In God they can find all the strength they need to follow him in every area of their lives. Let's never give up in encouraging our daughters and covering them in prayer.

– 37 –

When She's Finding Her Identity

Do not love the world or anything in the world. If anyone loves the world, love for the Father is not in them. For everything in the world—the lust of the flesh, the lust of the eyes, and the pride of life—comes not from the Father but from the world. The world and its desires pass away, but whoever does the will of God lives forever.

1 John 2:15–17

But you are a chosen people, a royal priesthood, a holy nation, God's special possession, that you may declare the praises of him who called you out of darkness into his wonderful light.

1 Peter 2:9

Lord,

I thank you for the amazing new identity you have given my daughter. You call her your child and your friend. You promise her an inheritance and reward. You declare her to be holy and righteous and are transforming her into a new creation. You offer "every spiritual blessing" (Eph. 1:3), a new mind, and grace to endure anything that comes her way.

I pray that you would open her eyes to the love and gifts you have poured out for her. May she have assurance, through and through, that *you* are her reason for life and joy. Be my daughter's first love so that nothing in this world can compare.

Give my daughter a heart to please you rather than the world around her. Keep her devoted to following your ways instead of the popular values or philosophies of the culture. May your gifts be more precious than any material thing she can see with her eyes.

Let her be devoted to glorifying you and making your name great instead of drawing attention to herself and seeking her own greatness. May her gratitude for all you've done create a humble, generous spirit that cares for others.

Thank you for giving my daughter a hope and a future. May she love you more and more all the days of her life. Amen.

– 38 –

When She Needs Community

But you are a chosen people, a royal priesthood, a holy nation, God's special possession, that you may declare the praises of him who called you out of darkness into his wonderful light. Once you were not a people, but now you are the people of God; once you had not received mercy, but now you have received mercy.

1 Peter 2:9–10

And let us consider how we may spur one another on toward love and good deeds, not giving up meeting together, as some are in the habit of doing, but encouraging one another—and all the more as you see the Day approaching.

Hebrews 10:24–25

Father,

Thank you for your church, the body of Christ. You've given us a place to belong in a family that will last for eternity. We can share our struggles and celebrations with others who follow you.

I pray that my daughter would find her place in your church. Bring believers around her to encourage her when she's struggling or losing her way. Use the love she sees in other Christians to testify to the way you care for her.

Protect her from the hurt and confusion that come when your people are absent or unfaithful. Give her wisdom to see that although you are perfect, people still fail and abandon what they say they believe. Don't allow the weakness she sees in others to cause doubt in her mind about your power and goodness.

Help her to find her true home in the body of Christ. Give her a sense of belonging and joy in caring for and serving your church. Give her the strength to stay present and involved. Create a sensitivity in her heart for other believers who are discouraged and need a friend to build them up. Create "cords" that are strong in hard times. May the world around her see those unique bonds and be drawn to you because of the love they see in her.

Thank you for giving us a community to lift us up while we wait for your return. You are so good to us and I love you. Amen.

– 39 –

When She's Rebellious

Do not be like the horse or the mule, which have no understanding but must be controlled by bit and bridle or they will not come to you. Many are the woes of the wicked, but the LORD's *unfailing love surrounds the one who trusts in him.*

Psalm 32:9–10

But I gave them this command: Obey me, and I will be your God and you will be my people. Walk in obedience to all I command you, that it may go well with you. But they did not listen or pay attention; instead, they followed the stubborn inclinations of their evil hearts. They went backward and not forward.

Jeremiah 7:23–24

Lord,

One of our greatest struggles is to submit to you. We want to go our own way, do our own thing, and answer to no one. We want to control our own destiny. We pick and choose which sins to tolerate in our lives—but are quick to criticize the behavior of everyone else! We feel torn in two; we want to follow you and love you, but our sinful desires pull us away.

Lord, be my daughter's rock. Be her unchangeable standard for right and wrong. Give her a heart that bends to your will and authority. Teach her to seek you before she runs toward a new relationship, opportunity, or temptation.

You say that rebellion against you brings foolishness and trouble into our lives. I love my daughter and want a life of blessing and peace for her. Help her to receive your love and salvation so she can trust you completely with her life. May she move forward into the future with you instead of turning aside to go her own way.

Keep my daughter from believing the lie that she should live her way, for herself. Silence the ones who teach her to despise authority. Who see submission as weak. Who think that we "only go around once" so she should gratify herself while she can. Open her eyes to see you! May she know your voice as her loving Shepherd who leads her into perfect rest and peace.

I know that someday every knee will bow and every tongue confess that Jesus Christ is Lord (Phil. 2:10–11). May my daughter and I trust in you *now*. Let us be surrendered in all things to you until Christ comes. Amen.

– 40 –

When She's Bored

This is the day that the LORD has made; let us rejoice and be glad in it.

Psalm 118:24 ESV

For we are God's handiwork, created in Christ Jesus to do good works, which God prepared in advance for us to do.

Ephesians 2:10

A person can do nothing better than to eat and drink and find satisfaction in their own toil. This too, I see, is from the hand of God, for without him who can eat or find enjoyment? To the person who pleases him, God gives wisdom, knowledge and happiness.

Ecclesiastes 2:24–26

Lord,

There is nothing worse on a quiet afternoon than my daughter coming to me and saying, "I'm bored!" So much of her time is spoken for, whether in school or other activities, that when she has a few free hours she can be lost as to how to spend them.

Help my daughter to find purpose in her days. Energize her to use her creativity. Burden her heart to want to serve her family and be helpful in our home. Give her an open spirit that welcomes friends and shows hospitality. Motivate her to expand her mind through reading and challenging games.

Show my daughter that you have purposes for her even though she's young. Give her anticipation each morning for how you will use her that day. Help her to see time as a gift from you, something not to be wasted but to be enjoyed to the fullest.

Give me wisdom in how to guide my daughter. Keep me from the trap of trying to entertain her every moment. Show me when to give her space to fill her own hours and when to draw near and have time together.

Fill my daughter's heart with gratitude for her wonderful life. Help her to count her blessings so she doesn't dwell on what she isn't able to do. Protect her from a negative attitude that makes her never feel satisfied. Let her see that her life is yours and that you desire to fill each day with good things.

Lord, when I'm tempted to say, "I'm bored," help me to be still and remember that I'm yours too. Let me stay cheerful and active so my daughter can see what joy can be found in living life to the fullest. Amen.

– 41 –

When She's Feeling Bitter

Get rid of all bitterness, rage and anger, brawling and slander, along with every form of malice. Be kind and compassionate to one another, forgiving each other, just as in Christ God forgave you.

Ephesians 4:31–32

Don't have anything to do with foolish and stupid arguments, because you know they produce quarrels. And the Lord's servant must not be quarrelsome but must be kind to everyone, able to teach, not resentful.

2 Timothy 2:23–24

See to it that no one falls short of the grace of God and that no bitter root grows up to cause trouble and defile many.

Hebrews 12:15

Therefore, as God's chosen people, holy and dearly loved, clothe yourselves with compassion, kindness, humility, gentleness and patience. Bear with each other and forgive one another if any of you has a grievance against someone. Forgive as the Lord forgave you.

Colossians 3:12–13

Lord,

When my daughter is offended or betrayed, the wounds can be deep. She may resolve to forgive someone but have a long struggle to forget the painful memory. Cutting words can echo in her mind for years after they are spoken. An insult can create feelings of embarrassment that never seem to fade. Sometimes her wounds don't heal but become resentment and bitterness that take deep root in her heart.

You know the hurt my daughter experienced. It wasn't fair or right. The relationship is broken and seems beyond repair. She's wondering if she can ever trust people the same way again.

Protect my daughter from holding a grudge. If bitterness grows in her heart, it will separate her from your grace. It will harden her toward others. She will struggle with anger and negativity. She will be so caught up in having justice, or what she thinks she deserves, that she'll lose her compassion for others.

Give her the strength to truly forgive. Guard her from slandering the other person or gossiping so that division doesn't spread. Help her to see her own weaknesses so she can be humble and understanding. Comfort her with your great love so that any offense seems light by comparison.

It's hard to see my precious daughter hurting. Please heal her wounds, fill her with your grace, and set her free from a bitter spirit. Thank you for your mercy that always forgives and lets us begin again. We love you. Amen.

A Dad's Story

I have noticed, as a dad of girls, that it is much easier to give in to fear than it is to "be strong and courageous." That powerful phrase was said by God four times in the opening chapter of Joshua, as God prepared him for taking the leadership of an entire people after Moses's death. And that phrase is one I've been learning to live—and to pray for my daughters—for nearly seventeen years now.

I've heard it said that courage isn't the absence of fear, but rather courage is the willingness to do the right thing even in the face of fear. I've come to learn that the right thing in the face of fear is often more about trusting God than it is simply about "doing something." And that's a lesson I'm praying my girls will learn and live out.

But I've also been learning that in order for me to pass this courage on, God has to give me those opportunities first, so I can understand it and model it. This has played itself out most often when it comes to the helpless feelings we have had at times with the health of our daughters.

You see, I don't have just one daughter to pray for . . . I have eight daughters.

That's right. No sons. Eight daughters. Each a blessing. Each a joy. And each an opportunity to scare the living daylights out of me. And so I pray for the courage to trust God.

The Lord has been giving me opportunities for *years* to learn what trusting him, in the face of fear, looks like. Sometimes I have handled it well, by God's grace. Other times I have caved to the fear, even if only for a brief season. But in each case I have been learning that God is faithful and patient, and that my daughters are watching and learning from me (even when my mouth isn't open to "teach" them). Here are just a few examples . . .

My oldest, Hannah, did not like any sort of doctor's office when she was little. So when we had a traumatic dental visit when she was a little girl, I spent a lot of time with her, trying to comfort her and pray with her and for her. Imagine my surprise when, after some time waiting, the staff came in to tell us they would not treat her (even though she had calmed down).

Grrrrrrrr.

Well, we found a new dentist and, over time, my daughter has developed a stronger trust in the Lord that has helped her endure a tonsillectomy, many orthodontia visits, and even a complex broken ankle surgery and recovery. She's gaining the courage to trust God in the uncertainty of the doctor's office.

Now that is part of my daughter's heritage: to see how the Lord has helped me—and her—move beyond her fears and place herself in the care of another, just like we have to do with God every day.

When we were pregnant with Emma, our third daughter, we were warned in an early test that there was a possibility she would have Down Syndrome. We were asked if we wanted a more complex and possibly dangerous test to determine it with certainty. We declined, grateful that we had a heads-up about the possibility but knowing that the answer wouldn't change our course of action one single iota.

We used the months leading up to delivery not to ask God to keep her from having Down Syndrome, but to prepare our hearts and minds and lives for that possibility. When she was born, the cord was constricted during labor, providing even more tense, "this is out of my control" moments. More prayer. More courage needed to trust God. She made it through the delivery, and we rejoiced, not because she did not have Down

Syndrome, but because she was alive and because we were ready by God's grace for whatever came next.

And now that is part of my daughter's heritage: to know that the Lord was preparing our hearts to love and care for her, no matter what may come.

When we found out we were expecting our fourth child, Olivia, the timing could not have been more difficult. I had recently lost my job when my employer closed the company and declared bankruptcy. My grandmother, to whom I was very close, was dying of lung cancer nine hundred miles away. And I had to have surgery to remove a benign bone tumor above my left ankle.

I literally could not "pound the pavement" to even look for a job, much less travel to Missouri to visit my grandmother. But through the many hard days of that time period, God gave us the grace to endure, to put one foot in front of the other, to walk through the grief with my family, and to be open to the new adventure that he quickly provided.

It was hard. It was dark. But it was good.

And now that is part of my daughter's heritage: to know that the wonderful news of her life came in a hard time that God was able to see us through.

It seems to be a theme in my life: God asks me over and over again, *Am I enough for you?*

So now this has become part of my prayers for my eight daughters. *Lord*, I ask, *please help me to show my daughters what it* looks *like to walk by faith, to trust in you, even when I can't see a way out or I don't know how you'll do what you want and need to do. Please help them to have the courage they need to trust you, no matter what, beyond their circumstances.*

Leon C. Wirth, executive director of parenting
and youth at Focus on the Family

When She's Lonely

The LORD himself goes before you and will be with you; he will never leave you nor forsake you. Do not be afraid; do not be discouraged.

Deuteronomy 31:8

And surely I am with you always, to the very end of the age.

Matthew 28:20

Where can I go from your Spirit? Where can I flee from your presence? If I go up to the heavens, you are there; if I make my bed in the depths, you are there. If I rise on the wings of the dawn, if I settle on the far side of the sea, even there your hand will guide me, your right hand will hold me fast.

Psalm 139:7–10

Father,

There are times when we feel alone in this world. Close friends and family move away. We change jobs, homes, and schools and find ourselves in unfamiliar places, on the outside looking in. Relationships grow apart, or we feel that no one in our circle really knows us well or cares to deepen the friendship. We can suffer betrayal and rejection and become completely isolated.

You know my daughter's pain of loneliness. Kids might act friendly at the lunch table but don't invite her to spend time outside of school. Her phone stays silent and the email inbox sits empty. She feels invisible and insecure.

Thank you for being my daughter's faithful friend. Even though she can't see you with her eyes, help her to *know* that you are by her side. May she use this season of aloneness to reach out to you. Let her hear your voice when she prays. Speak to her by your Spirit so she can experience your presence. Give her hope that you know her needs and will bring a special friend at just the right time.

Please give my daughter an open, friendly attitude toward others. Don't allow discouragement to harden her heart to reaching out. Bring a caring girl her way who will offer true and open friendship to her.

Show me how to be her companion during this season. Don't let me become so caught up in my own interests that I crowd her out. Help me to be fun and approachable—use this time to strengthen our bond to each other.

Thank you for your faithful care for my daughter. You are in control, and I trust you to protect her lonely heart and meet all her needs. Amen.

– 43 –

When She Needs to Pray

In the same way, the Spirit helps us in our weakness. We do not know what we ought to pray for, but the Spirit himself intercedes for us through wordless groans.

Romans 8:26

I call on you, my God, for you will answer me; turn your ear to me and hear my prayer.

Psalm 17:6

Rejoice always, pray continually, give thanks in all circumstances; for this is God's will for you in Christ Jesus.

1 Thessalonians 5:16–18

Lord,

Before Jesus returned to heaven, his disciples asked him to teach them how to pray (Luke 11:1). Give my daughter the same desire, and instruct her in how to talk with you. Show her that prayer isn't a formula or something we recite just to go through the motions. You want her to draw near to you, not just saying grace at meals and "thank you for this day" at bedtime.

Give her strength by your Spirit to make time to talk to you. Show her how to sit quietly with you until she hears your voice. Give her confidence that she is heard and not just talking to the ceiling. Give her a sense of expectancy that she will see you respond when she reaches out to you.

Prompt my daughter to want to share every part of her life with you in prayer. When she receives an award or overcomes a challenge, let her be excited to tell her heavenly Dad and praise you! When she's sick, tired, or discouraged, may she run to you for strength. When she loses something or someone precious, let her lean on you for comfort and help. May prayer become as natural as breathing for her, as she shares her day with you moment by moment.

Thank you for your great love that invites us to meet you in prayer. May my daughter discover that incredible gift. Amen.

– 44 –

When She Needs Discipline

"My son, do not regard lightly the discipline of the Lord, nor be weary when reproved by him. For the Lord disciplines the one he loves, and chastises every son whom he receives." It is for discipline that you have to endure. God is treating you as sons. For what son is there whom his father does not discipline? If you

are left without discipline, in which all have participated, then you are illegitimate children and not sons. Besides this, we have had earthly fathers who disciplined us and we respected them. Shall we not much more be subject to the Father of spirits and live? For they disciplined us for a short time as it seemed best to them, but he disciplines us for our good, that we may share his holiness. For the moment all discipline seems painful rather than pleasant, but later it yields the peaceful fruit of righteousness to those who have been trained by it.

Hebrews 12:5–11 ESV

Father,

You are kind and patient with my weaknesses. Thank you for loving me so much that you correct me when I need it. You bring me back into a right relationship with you, and you show me how to live in your will so I can experience all of your goodness.

Teach me how to discipline my daughter. I often care too much about her pleasing me and chastise her for disrupting my plans or preferences. Help me to guide her in pleasing *you* instead of just myself. Show me what needs correction in her life so I can teach her your ways. Use my discipline to keep her from stumbling and becoming overtaken by sin.

Show me how to discipline her with love. May my words be full of truth and kindness. Let the consequences of her actions be fair and right. Help me to be gentle and protect her heart even as I hold her accountable for her behavior.

Help my daughter to receive correction with a humble spirit. Soften her heart to be able to admit her faults. Let her love for you create repentance, and let her love for me create trust that I'm on her side.

Use times of correction as a way to bond us together. Make me her helper as she learns to follow you in every area of her life. Give me a forgiving spirit if she lets me down or offends me so that no resentment builds up between us. Give her a gracious spirit toward me even if my decisions are hard for her to understand.

Cover us with your grace. Let us "throw off everything that hinders and the sin that so easily entangles" (Heb. 12:1) so we can grow in faith and become more like Jesus. Amen.

– 45 –

When She Needs Modesty

Your beauty should not come from outward adornment, such as elaborate hairstyles and the wearing of gold jewelry or fine clothes. Rather, it should be that of your inner self, the unfading beauty of a gentle and quiet spirit, which is of great worth in God's sight. For this is the way the holy women of the past who put their hope in God used to adorn themselves.

1 Peter 3:3–5

Charm is deceptive, and beauty is fleeting; but a woman who fears the LORD is to be praised.

Proverbs 31:30

Father,

The world is sending a destructive message to my daughter, that she should draw as much attention to herself as possible by her appearance. Young girls are encouraged to dress like grown women. Worse, they are pressured to look sexy rather than feminine and lovely as you created them.

Models and actresses present a confusing example of how my daughter should present herself. They imply she should focus on fashion and image and stay constantly in style at the risk of being inferior. She's given the impression that she'll be loved for her sexuality rather than her loving spirit and personality, and that she has to be overtly outgoing and attention-getting to be noticed.

Guard my daughter's mind from these lies. Let her be content to please you in every way, even in how she presents herself physically. Give her peace and security through modest clothing and a quiet spirit. May she be concerned with delighting her heavenly Father rather than trying to attract the notice of boys who can never love her like you.

Help my daughter to put her energy into developing her inner self—seeking wisdom, gentleness, and joy. Allow her modesty and sweetness to reveal how beautiful you are in her life. Thank you for giving my daughter a hope the world doesn't understand. Amen.

Her Failures

For the righteous falls seven times and rises again, but the wicked stumble in times of calamity.

Proverbs 24:16 ESV

Sum up the life of Jesus by any other standard than God's, and it is an anticlimax of failure.

Oswald Chambers[6]

Most of us at some point are struck with a fear of failure. Our identities are so wrapped up in our success that we end up investing all our energy and attention in it. We feel we have to get the part, make the team, get into the college of our choice, find our dream job, marry the most desirable woman, and never stop until we obtain our passion in life. We put so much pressure on ourselves to have it all that we'll fight for it at any cost.

Once we become fathers, we place that same kind of drive onto our daughters. My daughter can believe she'll find the secret to life (and the way to win her dad's heart) if she can find the way to be the best. How does she describe her failures? Does she say, "I guess that didn't work out too well, but I'll keep trying and maybe it will go better next time," or does she slander her own character with, "I'm such a loser! I'm never going to get it right!"? Her words may reveal what she's believing in her heart about where her worth really comes from.

As dads, we need to let our girls know a few things. First, failure is universal! "For all have sinned and fall short of the glory of God" (Rom. 3:23). Every person on the planet will betray his or her own conscience and do the wrong thing. We can't hope for perfection until Jesus returns and completes his work of making us new. Until then, I need to let my daughter know she can always find forgiveness with us and with the Lord. My prayer is she'll take hold of the truth that "there is now no condemnation for those who are in Christ Jesus" (8:1).

The second thing to teach our daughters is that failure is never wasted. God promises to take every situation and work it "for the good of those who love him, who have been called according to his purpose" (v. 28). Sometimes we really do learn the most the hard way. My daughter doesn't always do her homework and clean her room just because her mother or I tell her to. She might need a bad grade on an exam or a lost iPod buried in the mess in her closet to learn self-discipline and obedience.

Finally, our daughters need to know that we're not going to rescue them from every failure. That can be hard for us dads because we love to be the hero! If I "help" her finish a book report by taking over and writing it myself, I'm compromising my integrity and hindering her education. If I pay for the extra charges on the phone bill because she didn't pay attention to her texting limit, I'm keeping her from learning responsibility. If I try to pull strings to get her a place on the team even though she didn't pass the tryouts, I'm fostering a selfish sense of entitlement. I need to get out of the way sometimes, so God can use her failures to grow my daughter to maturity.

Our daughters need to be convinced that love isn't something they earn. We're all hardwired to try to work for God's favor through our behavior. We fall into living by a set of rules to feel righteous, instead of trusting in the completed work of Jesus on the cross to make us right before God. I do the same with my daughter—obey me, please me, impress me, and I'll give you affection and attention. Fail, and you'll see my disapproval as I keep you at arm's length. God wants to reveal himself to my daughter through my own unconditional love. When I'm forgiving and accepting of my girl no matter how she's fallen, she sees God's kind of love right before her eyes.

I don't love my daughter because she's awesome (although I think she is!). I love her because she's mine. God doesn't love us because we're perfect. He loves us because we're his chosen people, created to be with him forever. May we give our daughters grace to fail without the fear of losing our heart.

– 46 –

When She Needs to Serve

Whoever wants to become great among you must be your servant, and whoever wants to be first must be slave of all. For even the Son of Man did not come to be served, but to serve, and to give his life as a ransom for many.

Mark 10:43–45

Be devoted to one another in love. Honor one another above yourselves. Never be lacking in zeal, but keep your spiritual fervor, serving the Lord. Be joyful in hope, patient in affliction, faithful in prayer. Share with the Lord's people who are in need. Practice hospitality.

Romans 12:10–13

And do not forget to do good and to share with others, for with such sacrifices God is pleased.

Hebrews 13:16

Father,

Thank you for giving us new life! You have rescued us from the hopeless road of living only for ourselves. You have given us purpose and meaning in serving and loving those around us.

Teach my daughter what it means to be a servant. Reveal to her the mystery that putting others first and showing generosity end up bringing us incredible satisfaction. Deepen her knowledge of Christ as she sees Christians serve and sacrifice for others.

Give my daughter open hands to share what she has. Soften her heart for those who are struggling—create a compassionate spirit that prompts her to run to help. Bring opportunities her way to practice hospitality and giving.

Use our home as a place to learn these values. Use me as an example, by the way I invite others to share meals with us and look for ways to help our neighbors. Show me where to give and serve your people so my daughter can see my faith in action.

Make us willing to lay down our own comforts and convenience to help anyone you bring our way. Keep us from withholding anything you may ask us to give, for your glory. Amen.

– 47 –

When She Can Share Her Faith

I am not ashamed of the gospel, because it is the power of God that brings salvation to everyone who believes: first to the Jew, then to the Gentile.

Romans 1:16

You are the light of the world. A town built on a hill cannot be hidden. Neither do people light a lamp and put it under a bowl. Instead they put it on its stand, and it gives light to everyone in the house. In the same way, let your light shine before others, that they may see your good deeds and glorify your Father in heaven.

Matthew 5:14–16

In your hearts revere Christ as Lord. Always be prepared to give an answer to everyone who asks you to give the reason for the hope that you have.

1 Peter 3:15

Lord,

You promise that someday "every knee should bow, in heaven and on earth and under the earth, and every tongue acknowledge that Jesus Christ is Lord, to the glory of God the Father" (Phil. 2:10–11). We long for that day to come—to see all of mankind declaring that you are worthy of praise! It breaks our hearts that so many around us have never heard of your love and are lost, without hope or a future.

Help my daughter to discover the power of the gospel. Let your salvation transform her and fill her with your light. May her life bring praise to you as she lives and loves like Jesus. Give her so much joy in being your child that it spills over onto everyone she knows.

Give my daughter confidence to speak of the One she is trusting. Let her praise you when good things happen each day. May she give you the glory for her successes as you give her strength. May she express peace and hope even in difficult times, knowing that you are in control and will work everything for her good in the end. Let her be ready to explain her devotion to you when others question her choices.

Give her compassion for friends and family who don't know you. Teach her to pray persistently for their salvation, believing you will move through her prayers. As she cares for those around her, let them experience a taste of how much you care for them too.

Thank you for loving this world so much. You don't turn away but continue to shine your light into the darkest places. May my daughter and I let our light shine before everyone without holding back. Come soon, Lord Jesus. Amen.

– 48 –

When She's Unique and Special

Train a child in the way he should go, and even when he is old he will not turn away from it.

Proverbs 22:6 GW

You have searched me, LORD, and you know me. You know when I sit and when I rise; you perceive my thoughts from afar. You discern my going out and my lying down; you are familiar with all my ways.

Psalm 139:1–3

Father,

You know my daughter so intimately. You know what motivates her. What gifts and talents are waiting to develop. Whether she's a morning person or a night owl. How introverted or extroverted she is around others. What flavors of ice cream and varieties of animals she enjoys. How she likes to express herself. What her dreams are for the future. You know her even better than I do.

Give me insight to know my daughter more and more each day. Help me to understand her well so I can direct her in the path that's just right for her unique personality. Make me a student of my daughter—to listen, observe, and enjoy each quality you have created in her wonderful self.

Keep me from trying to shape her into what *I* want her to be. If she's an athlete instead of a musician, let me be willing to support her wholeheartedly. If she's quiet and reserved, may I be at peace even if she isn't the center of attention. If she's creative and artistic, give me patience when her math homework is a struggle!

Remind me continually that my daughter was made in *your* image, not mine. Help me to value what you have created even in the areas we are different. Fill me with grace for my daughter, so I can love and cherish her with all my heart. Thank you for loving us so fully just the way we are. Amen.

A Dad's Story

I majored in mathematics in college. I like formulas. I like being able to solve problems with proven techniques and proofs. I like concise, elegant, and boxed answers. Ironically, in my short time here on this planet, I have quickly learned of at least two things that don't fit nice, neat formulas: life and daughters. In addition, if you have chosen to trust the God of the Bible, then you must be willing to accept not understanding why things happen at times. These issues are quite difficult for math majors.

My daughter is quickly growing into a beautiful young woman. She is compassionate, competent, attractive, graceful, type A, and ready to take on the world. As an accomplished young dancer, she is extremely beautiful to watch and has been told so over the years. On the outside, it appears most things are going her way and that life has come pretty easy for her. In some regards, that is true. However, it would be naive to believe that "everything" is going well for a young teen no matter what the outside looks like. Furthermore, sometimes life throws us nasty curveballs that buckle our knees and shake our confidence. This pitch came directly for my daughter, out of nowhere, and presented her with unforeseen challenges. I have been praying for my daughter's heart, health, development, and identity since the day she was born. In the same way my daughter's life was about to change, my prayers for her were about to change dramatically as well.

As I mentioned previously, my daughter is an accomplished dancer and dreams of dancing professionally. Unfortunately, in the span of fourteen months she severely injured her ankle, persevered through three months of inconclusive diagnosis appointments, underwent surgery, missed her studio's main performance, attended her dear great grandmother's funeral, rehabilitated her ankle and returned to dancing, and then re-injured her ankle. Thoughts of *Will it ever heal?* began to creep in and shake her confidence.

In the midst of this ordeal, in a freak series of events, her best friend of ten years had an unexpected heart stoppage prior to a cross-country training run. The short version of the long story is that her friend's brain was without oxygen for a conservative estimate of ten to fifteen minutes—it may have been longer. She was taken immediately to a nearby children's hospital with my daughter and wife not far behind. My daughter spent the next week in the waiting room and other nooks and crannies waiting to see if her best friend was going to live or die. Not just when she might recover, but if she was going to survive. On top of it, if she survived, questions arose as to the extent of brain damage that would exist. I can't even begin to imagine the severity of emotions and uncertainty my daughter faced during this time, especially as a young teenager.

Miraculously, my daughter's friend survived. It was determined she had a genetic heart issue and had no way of knowing her condition. In addition, she recovered with no apparent brain damage. In fact, she was over at our house just the other night eating dinner with us and telling jokes. She is a literal walking miracle.

In the midst of the joy of her friend's recovery, my daughter began experiencing signs of post-traumatic stress disorder, which developed during that week in the hospital. As a dad who thrives on formulas, control, and boxed answers, I was struggling mightily to see hope for my soon-to-be-sixteen-year-old daughter as she faced possible dashed dancing dreams, identity issues, the loss of her great grammy, the potential loss of her best friend, and now PTSD.

Prayer is a funny thing. I continue to wrestle with the concept of praying to an omnipotent God who asks us to bring our requests to him. Moving past that obvious tension is challenging for a former math major. But when curveballs begin humming at my daughter's head, I immediately fall to my knees begging for relief and hope. My original prayers for my daughter continue but are slightly different now. I pray more for her heart to understand God's trustworthiness even when we don't have a clue why nasty stuff happens. I pray for her strong health to return and for her childhood dreams to be realized, but I also pray for contentment in spite of circumstances. And above all, I pray that she might have a rock-solid understanding of her identity in Jesus so that she can embrace all life has to offer.

In many ways, God has responded in these more dramatic circumstances like he has throughout time. He seems to continually ask us, *Do you trust me?*, and sometimes in the midst of pain and great misunderstanding, he is silent. Then suddenly we witness a ray of hope—or even a miracle—reminding us who God is. I've often thought when God doesn't feel close it's usually not because he's moved away but because I have. In my experience, God is trustworthy, even when I don't have clarity as to why things happen.

Navigating the teenage years is rarely easy. Life in general is messy, and many times no easy, boxed answers exist. It is during these seasons that faith has an opportunity to stretch and grow, sometimes painfully, and solidify who God is. In the same way my daughter is growing, I am too. We're both learning to face knee-buckling curveballs with courage and trust in God.

Tracy Sims, associate pastor,
Grace Community Fellowship, Eugene, Oregon

− 49 −

When She's Using the Internet

Rob and Joanna Teigen

Be alert and of sober mind. Your enemy the devil prowls around like a roaring lion looking for someone to devour.

1 Peter 5:8

In his arrogance the wicked man hunts down the weak, who are caught in the schemes he devises. . . . Like a lion in cover he lies in wait. He lies in wait to catch the helpless; he catches the helpless and drags them off in his net. His victims are crushed, they collapse; they fall under his strength. He says to himself, "God will never notice; he covers his face and never sees."

Psalm 10:2, 9–11

Whoever dwells in the shelter of the Most High will rest in the shadow of the Almighty. I will say of the LORD*, "He is my refuge and my fortress, my God, in whom I trust." Surely he will save you from the fowler's snare and from the deadly pestilence. He will cover you with his feathers, and under his wings you will find refuge; his faithfulness will be your shield and rampart.*

Psalm 91:1–4

Lord,

The internet offers us an incredible means of finding information on any possible subject. We can use it to instantly connect with loved ones around the world. We can share our day-to-day experiences through social media and enjoy any type of music imaginable using online radio. It is also a wonderful means of sharing the gospel with those who have no access to Scripture or preaching from any other source.

Despite the array of benefits the internet offers, significant risks are present for my daughter when she goes online. She could experience gossip and bullying. She could be exposed to

109

pornography without even seeking it. Advertisers can create a false sense of need and foster materialism. Predators can try to lure my daughter into unthinkable sexual exploitation.

Protect my daughter from these dangers! Give her wisdom to know how to use the internet safely. Keep her from creating connections with anyone who might bring her pain or harm. Guard her eyes from anything that could steal her innocence. Teach her restraint about how much personal information she should share online.

The computer can be a trap that draws her in for hours, stealing her days and keeping her isolated from our family. Give me wisdom to know what boundaries to set, and give her a submissive heart to accept those limits. Create openness between us so she has no contacts or experiences online that are secret. Help me to know the best ways to support and protect her as she expands her world.

Thank you for your great love for my daughter. Thank you for watching over her in every moment. Continue to bless her with your presence and help in every situation. Amen.

– 50 –

When She's Dreaming about the Future

Take delight in the LORD and he will give you the desires of your heart. Commit your way to the LORD; trust in him and he will do this: He will make your righteous reward shine like the dawn, your vindication like the noonday sun.

Psalm 37:4–6

Commit to the LORD *whatever you do, and he will establish your plans. . . . In their hearts humans plan their course, but the* LORD *establishes their steps.*

Proverbs 16:3, 9

Trust in the LORD *with all your heart and lean not on your own understanding; in all your ways submit to him, and he will make your paths straight.*

Proverbs 3:5–6

Father,

One of the most exciting things about being a young girl is dreaming about the future. My daughter imagines all the careers she might pursue, where she could travel, the kind of person she might marry, and the talents and hobbies she might develop.

It's wonderful to know that you have dreams for her too. You already have a path for her life in mind. You have created her with gifts and talents and already know the opportunities that will come along for her to use them.

Give my daughter faith to believe in your wisdom and goodness. Help her to seek you first as she considers different goals and plans. Teach her that she can trust you—following your path will bring more joy and satisfaction than any dream she could create on her own.

Use me as an example of someone who follows you in life. Let me wait on you before I jump into any plan of action. Make me prayerful as I consider each decision that comes along. Give me confidence and enthusiasm when you open a door to a new experience, so she can see that following you is exciting.

May my daughter and I both love you, your ways, and your will above anything. Help us to seek you wholeheartedly and surrender our futures to your control. Thank you that we don't have to figure out life on our own. We can trust you and face each new day with confidence, knowing you go before us and will walk with us every step of the way. Amen.

– 51 –

When She Needs My Influence

Listen, my son, to your father's instruction and do not forsake your mother's teaching. They are a garland to grace your head and a chain to adorn your neck. . . . Listen to your father, who gave you life, and do not despise your mother when she is old.

Proverbs 1:8–9; 23:22

Listen, my son, accept what I say, and the years of your life will be many. I instruct you in the way of wisdom and lead you along straight paths. When you walk, your steps will not be hampered; when you run, you will not stumble. Hold on to instruction, do not let it go; guard it well, for it is your life.

Proverbs 4:10–13

Lord,

Many voices will compete for my daughter's ear, seeking to influence her opinions, values, and goals. She'll have teachers, friends, coaches, TV personalities, and all kinds of media speaking into her life. Some of these voices will encourage her to become independent and grow up way too fast. They may devalue your truth. They may counsel her to trust in her own immature insight rather than my teaching or input as her dad.

In all the "noise," please preserve my influence over my daughter's mind and heart. You provided her with a parent who loves her and is ready to lay down anything for her well-being. I desire to share my help, knowledge, and faith with her as she navigates the road toward adulthood.

Keep her heart soft toward me. Protect our relationship from distance or division. Keep us communicating well so we can talk over her day-to-day challenges. Give her a firm hold on wisdom and truth so she can recognize foolish advice when it comes her way.

Give me gentleness and self-control so I don't alienate my daughter. Make me a man of integrity so she can put her trust in me. Keep me from any behavior or choices that would ruin my credibility and influence in her life. Most of all, make me loving like you so she always feels treasured and secure.

Thank you for my daughter. It is a humbling privilege to be her father and I pray I will be faithful to her in everything. Bless and keep us in you. Amen.

– 52 –

When She Needs Comfort

Praise be to the God and Father of our Lord Jesus Christ, the Father of compassion and the God of all comfort, who comforts us in all our troubles, so that we can comfort those in any trouble with the comfort we ourselves receive from God.

2 Corinthians 1:3–4

I will glory in the LORD; let the afflicted hear and rejoice. . . . I sought the LORD, and he answered me; he delivered me from all my fears. . . . The LORD is close to the brokenhearted and saves those who are crushed in spirit.

Psalm 34:2, 4, 18

Father,

Sometimes we have a "terrible, horrible, no good, very bad day!" We have a headache. We fail a test. We lose our phone, our keys, or even our car in the parking lot. We spill lunch on our favorite shirt. We forget an appointment or let someone down who was counting on us. Or they let *us* down and we feel betrayed. We embarrass ourselves in front of our peers. Our bank account runs out before the bills are paid. The fun weekend plans we made break down at the last minute. We get in a petty argument that spoils the mood around the house for days.

In those times when it feels like nothing is going right, show my daughter what a comforter you are. Teach her to go to you with every little struggle instead of reaching out to you only in a crisis. Show her that you are beside her in every moment. Help her to lean on you so daily challenges don't have to drag her down and steal her joy. Give her courage that guards her heart from fear.

Lord, as she discovers help and compassion from you, use her to encourage those around her. When she bounces back from disappointment because of your comfort, use her cheerful spirit to lift up those who are struggling. Give her a grateful heart that creates a joyful, hopeful outlook—she will bring your light to others who are hurting in the dark.

Thank you for the compassion you show whenever we're in pain. You rescue us from fear and despair. When we feel like we can't go on, you share your hope and strength and we make it through another day. Help us to share the help and comfort you bless us with so everyone can know your great love. Amen.

– 53 –

When She's Depressed

My soul is weary with sorrow; strengthen me according to your word.

Psalm 119:28

A cheerful heart is good medicine, but a crushed spirit dries up the bones.

Proverbs 17:22

O LORD my God, I cried to you for help, and you have healed
me. . . . You have turned for me my mourning into dancing; you
have loosed my sackcloth and clothed me with gladness, that my
glory may sing your praise and not be silent. O LORD my God, I
will give thanks to you forever!

Psalm 30:2, 11–12 ESV

Father,

Sometimes life is painful. We are wounded by loss, disappointment, or betrayal by someone we trust. We experience crushing fatigue or burnout. A dream or hope we held for a long, long time comes to nothing.

Lord, it's natural for my daughter to hurt when she goes through those kinds of experiences. I pray, though, that she would not become snared by negative emotions and unable to find joy again. Protect my daughter's heart and mind from despair and depression.

Guard my daughter's thoughts from fixating on her pain. Instead, help her to remember her blessings and see all of the good in her life. Help her to recognize how much she is loved. How valued she is by her family and friends. Remind her that her troubles are temporary and new possibilities are right around the corner.

Keep my daughter from a negative, complaining spirit. Fill her with hope about the future. Help her to move past her hurt and disappointment and trust you to meet her every need. Let her find peace and contentment in the knowledge that you love her and will never leave her alone. Give her true joy that isn't just happiness in circumstances, but confidence in your faithfulness and goodness to her all the days of her life.

Thank you that you bring us through every pain and struggle. You are our life and our hope. Amen.

– 54 –

When She Needs Humility

For by the grace given me I say to every one of you: Do not think of yourself more highly than you ought, but rather think of yourself with sober judgment, in accordance with the faith God has distributed to each of you.

Romans 12:3

Do nothing out of selfish ambition or vain conceit. Rather, in humility value others above yourselves.

Philippians 2:3

All of you, clothe yourselves with humility toward one another, because, "God opposes the proud but shows favor to the humble." Humble yourselves, therefore, under God's mighty hand, that he may lift you up in due time.

1 Peter 5:5–6

Father,

There is constant pressure on my daughter to be amazing! So much of her life centers on performance, to be excellent at every course and activity she's involved in. Her self-worth can become wrapped up in her grades, popularity, and winning.

It's easy for my daughter to wrap up her identity and goals in performing well for others. And she can get caught up in the trap of comparing herself to the girls around her. If she's successful, she can feel superior to her friends and classmates, and if she's not, then she can become insecure and jealous.

Help my daughter to focus on pleasing you more than anyone else. Help her to use her gifts for your glory rather than her own. If she excels in a class, a sport, or the arts, prompt her to use those abilities to help others who aren't as strong. Teach her to cheer others on and celebrate their victories instead of craving attention just for herself. If she receives praise or awards, let her thank *you* for enabling her to do so well.

If my daughter struggles and finds that no matter how hard she tries she just can't be the best, help her to find peace. Give her contentment in how she was created. Show her that although she may have limitations in certain areas, you surely have gifted her in other ways that will come to light over time. Help her to appreciate the successes of her friends and siblings instead of falling into jealousy and resentment.

Thank you for guarding my daughter's heart from pride and shame. May she have a humble, loving spirit that blesses everyone she knows. May she know your peace as she works and grows in life as your child. Amen.

Her Protection

We are consumed by safety. Obsessed with it, actually. Now, I'm not saying it is wrong to pray for God's protection, but I am questioning how we've made safety our highest priority. We've elevated safety to the neglect of whatever God's best is.

Francis Chan[7]

f I'm honest, I don't always know how to relate to my daughter! I'm not always sure how to meet her needs. It can be confusing to understand what our relationship is supposed to look like. But despite all of my insecurities, I believe fathers know how to provide and protect. We have an inner drive to shelter our daughters from harm, and we want to be their hero.

When I look around and see all the threats to my daughter's safety, it can be overwhelming. The headlines describe violence, sexual predators, out-of-control viruses, a shaky economy, and a broken educational system. And closer to home, she can suffer from sickness, the betrayal of friends, bullying, academic failings, and her own weaknesses and temptations. It's hard as her dad to feel so powerless to protect her from everything that endangers her well-being.

Praise God that we can take all of our worries and fears to him. His Word encourages me when it says, "Be strong and courageous. Do not be afraid or terrified because of them, for the Lord your God goes with you; he will never leave you nor forsake you" (Deut. 31:6). He promises that he is mighty to save, a strong tower, an ever-present help in trouble, and the defender of the weak. With the God of the universe at our side, "I will not be afraid. What can mere mortals do to me?" (Heb. 13:6).

I'm encouraged that even when difficulties and crises do come our way, God promises he won't waste the pain. He'll use every trial to grow our faith and teach us to persevere. We'll discover parts of him we never knew before—his comfort, compassion, and strength in every situation. I know when I see my daughter in pain I wish I could take it for her. I'd rather be hurt myself than watch her go through it. So knowing that God is with us every moment, taking what the enemy intends for evil and using it for good, eases my mind and helps me find peace.

The real battleground when it comes to protecting my girl is my desire for control. It's hard knowing I can't create perfect safety for my children. No matter how many rules and restrictions I place in my daughter's life, she'll never be completely secure. I only find rest when I accept God's authority over our lives. Daniel 4:34–35 gives me the right perspective when it says, "His dominion is an eternal dominion; his kingdom endures from generation to generation. All the peoples of the earth are regarded as nothing. He does as he pleases with the powers of heaven and the peoples of the earth. No one can hold back his hand or say to him: 'What have you done?'" If I remember that God is God and I am not, I can place my daughter in his hands and release her future to him.

I am responsible for setting boundaries around my daughter with the wisdom God has given me. He uses me as his hand of protection in her life. It's important that I'm governed by the Spirit and not my own fears when it comes to setting limits. As she grows and becomes more independent, I don't always have the discernment to know how late she should stay out at night, whether she is ready for driver's training, which friends might be a negative influence, or if her school curriculum is blatantly contradicting the values she's been taught. Through prayer we find God's help in making these tough choices. I don't want to make rules by copying the choices of other dads, by passing down the habits I was raised with, or by what I think will make my daughter like me. I need God's help at all times to know how to best lead and protect my children.

Let's pray for God's wisdom to tell us when to release our daughters and give them more freedom, even if it's hard to let go. Our faith will grow as we trust God more and more for their protection. And let's pray for courage when he asks us to step in and say no because he reveals a threat to their physical, emotional, or spiritual security. When that happens I may lose some popularity with my daughter for a time, but I'll have the peace that comes from obeying our Father. Praise God that we don't have to parent in our own strength and understanding. He is faithful to help us and watch over our daughters every step of the way.

– 55 –

When She's Managing Her Money

Those who want to get rich fall into temptation and a trap and into many foolish and harmful desires that plunge people into ruin and destruction. For the love of money is a root of all kinds of evil. Some people, eager for money, have wandered from the faith and pierced themselves with many griefs.

1 Timothy 6:9–10

A wife of noble character who can find? She is worth far more than rubies. . . . She considers a field and buys it; out of her earnings she plants a vineyard. She sets about her work vigorously; her arms are strong for her tasks. She sees that her trading is profitable, and her lamp does not go out at night.

Proverbs 31:10, 16–18

No one can serve two masters. Either you will hate the one and love the other, or you will be devoted to the one and despise the other. You cannot serve both God and money.

Matthew 6:24

Lord God,

Money can be a blessing and a trap at the same time. We work hard, and it is a right reward for our efforts. We use it to sustain our household and meet our physical needs. We share it with others to relieve suffering and do your work in the world. However, it can bring temptation, and we can get caught up in thinking we need more and more of it to be happy.

I pray that you would give my daughter a right perspective on money. Help her to recognize your provision for her and praise you. Help her to be content with what she has and not believe the lie that money can buy happiness. Protect her from a greedy spirit that always wants more and hates to share.

Give her the wisdom and strength to work hard and save her earnings. As she grows, give her creativity and diligence to find ways to build her bank account. May she have the self-control to spend her money wisely—keep her from impulsive shopping that squanders instead of saves.

Give my daughter a generous spirit so she gives cheerfully. Let her see everything she has as coming from your hand. While it's wise to save, keep her from a hoarding mentality and from finding security in her bank balance instead of you.

Use me as an example in the way I handle my finances. Let me be diligent in my work, mindful of my spending, content

120

with what I have, and generous to everyone. Give me a grateful heart for all of my material possessions.

Thank you for providing for me and my family so faithfully. May we always love you instead of just the blessings you have given. Amen.

– 56 –

When She Considers Dating

Above all else, guard your heart, for everything you do flows from it.

Proverbs 4:23

Flee the evil desires of youth and pursue righteousness, faith, love and peace, along with those who call on the Lord out of a pure heart.

2 Timothy 2:22

And this is my prayer: that your love may abound more and more in knowledge and depth of insight, so that you may be able to discern what is best and may be pure and blameless for the day of Christ.

Philippians 1:9–10

Father,

My daughter's heart and purity are treasures worth keeping and protecting. You have created her to be a beautiful gift to our family, her friends, and any man she chooses to love someday.

Teach my daughter to value her own heart. Help her to guard it well, not sharing herself emotionally or physically with anyone before the proper time. Give her wisdom in dating and in building friendships based on kindness and respect. Keep her from commitments to anyone who will tear her down or steal what should be saved for her husband.

Give my daughter peace and confidence in your love for her and mine. Fill her heart so she doesn't need the affection or attention of a boy to make her feel valuable or complete. Help her to keep her relationships in balance so that dating doesn't crowd out her friendships or family time.

Let my daughter's dating life prepare her for marriage someday. Use it to teach her discernment about the qualities she enjoys and values in others. Help her stand up to pressure to commit too deeply, too early. May she be cared for and protected like a sister by any young man who wants to spend time with her.

Help me to set wise boundaries around my daughter's dating experiences. Give us a close relationship so I can have insight and influence in this area. Help me to make my decisions based not on fear but on your wisdom alone. Teach me to encourage and support my daughter as she grows up and prepares her heart for her husband. Make my love for her so faithful and full of grace that it becomes her right standard for how she should be loved for a lifetime.

Thank you for my daughter and her beautiful heart. Amen.

– 57 –

When She Needs a Friend

Do not be yoked together with unbelievers. For what do righteousness and wickedness have in common? Or what fellowship can light have with darkness?

2 Corinthians 6:14

The righteous choose their friends carefully, but the way of the wicked leads them astray.

Proverbs 12:26

Two are better than one, because they have a good return for their labor: If either of them falls down, one can help the other up. But pity anyone who falls and has no one to help them up. Also, if two lie down together, they will keep warm. But how can one keep warm alone? Though one may be overpowered, two can defend themselves. A cord of three strands is not quickly broken.

Ecclesiastes 4:9–12

Father,

Navigating friendships and social pressures is difficult for my daughter. Her heart longs for acceptance and a sense of belonging with other girls. It would be so easy for her to sacrifice positive relationships for the sake of fitting in.

I pray that you would give the gift of friendship to my daughter. Bring a kind, gracious girl into her life who will be an encouragement to her. Help her to find a friend who is committed to you so they can walk in their faith together. Allow her to have a friend with whom she can be herself and find complete acceptance.

Give my daughter and her friends eyes to see past the surface, to appreciate each other's personalities and character and not just their appearance. Help them to live by your standards—to be honest, free from gossip, forgiving, kind, and pure. Teach them to encourage one another and show loyalty when one is having a difficult time. May they be open and friendly to others and set an example of goodness to the kids around them.

Give my daughter patience to wait for the right friends rather than rushing into unhealthy relationships to avoid feeling alone. Give her strength so she doesn't just follow the crowd but stays true to what she knows is right. Help her to know you as her friend and become like you in the way she cares for others.

Thank you for my daughter's heart and the blessing she is to those who know her. May she be blessed in her friendships and feel your love through the people in her life. Amen.

– 58 –

When She Needs a Mentor

Let us hold unswervingly to the hope we profess, for he who promised is faithful. And let us consider how we may spur one another on toward love and good deeds.

Hebrews 10:23–24

Likewise, teach the older women to be reverent in the way they live, not to be slanderers or addicted to much wine, but to teach what is good. Then they can urge the younger women to love their husbands and children, to be self-controlled and pure, to be busy at home, to be kind, and to be subject to their husbands, so that no one will malign the word of God.

Titus 2:3–5

Lord,

Growing up is too complicated for my daughter to handle alone. She faces so many changes in herself and her life from year to year that she can experience fear and confusion. As school and social pressures bear down on her, it's easy to forget your love and wisdom.

In your wonderful design, you intend for my daughter to receive counsel and encouragement from older women. I pray that you would bring godly women into her life who are willing to care for her as she grows. Inspire church leaders, teachers, coaches, and friends' mothers to pursue a close relationship with my daughter. Equip her mother with wisdom and energy to guide her no matter how busy our weeks become.

Lord, I pray you will handpick just the right women to have influence over my daughter's dreams and choices. Use them to reveal your great love. Fill their words with truth and wisdom. Create laughter and affection that soften my daughter to share her heart. Allow special memories to be created, so when difficult times come along my daughter remembers who is truly there for her.

Give me wisdom to know how to support her relationships with other women. Show me when to provide time, money, and encouragement for them to connect. Let me serve my family in a way that frees my wife to take time away with our daughter. Help me to build my wife up in her faith so she has spiritual resources to share.

I know I can't be all things to my daughter. Thank you for your good Word, which reminds me of my daughter's need for older women in her life. Help me to trust you to grow her in every way in your perfect timing. Amen.

A Dad's Story

Early on in our ministry, when our kids were small, we were living on one of those shoestring budgets. There was always too much month left at the end of the money. So our family would often pray together, asking God to supply our needs. I have a bucket load of stories as to how God answered our prayers, and as I look back now, I'm convinced that he did those things to build the faith of our children when they were very young so that they would always remember that he is a God who cares and provides for us.

In those days, buying new clothes for our growing daughter was an economic challenge, particularly since a lot of her friends wore pretty spiffy clothes. And, since Libby was our only daughter, there was no hope of hand-me-downs from an older sister. One day, much to our surprise, a box arrived from Cleveland, Ohio, from one of my wife's old friends. Her family had no clue what our family had been praying about, yet inside the box were several sets of clothes for a little girl. Not just any outfits but outfits with designer labels that represented the avant-garde of kids' fashion! I can still remember Libby jumping with joy when she saw the clothes, and they fit just right. The family continued to send boxes for several years filled with clothes from their daughter who obviously was just ahead of Libby in terms of size.

God had used prayer to give Libby an over-and-above blessing in her time of need. To this day she still remembers the impact of that prayer!

Joe Stowell,
president of Cornerstone University,
Grand Rapids, Michigan

– 59 –

When She's Being Bullied

You have heard that it was said, "Love your neighbor and hate your enemy." But I tell you, love your enemies and pray for those who persecute you, that you may be children of your Father in heaven.

Matthew 5:43–45

Contend, O LORD, with those who contend with me; fight against those who fight against me. Take up shield and armor; arise and

come to my aid. . . . They repay me evil for good and leave me
like one bereaved.

Psalm 35:1–2, 12

Turn to me and be gracious to me, for I am lonely and afflicted.
Relieve the troubles of my heart and free me from my anguish.
Look on my affliction and my distress and take away all my sins.
See how numerous are my enemies and how fiercely they hate
me! Guard my life and rescue me; do not let me be put to shame,
for I take refuge in you. May integrity and uprightness protect
me, because my hope, LORD, is in you.

Psalm 25:16–21

Almighty God,

My daughter has enemies even though she's just a child.
She suffers through bullying and mean-spirited treatment, and
nothing she does seems to relieve the struggle. Discouragement
and fear are setting in—she needs your help!

As her dad, I want to protect her from every kind of harm.
I get angry and want to pay back anyone who hurts my little
girl. It's frustrating when I can't watch over her every moment
or fix this painful situation.

Thank you that your name is a strong tower that she can
run to and be safe (Prov. 18:10). Come to my daughter's side
and defend her from those who are trying to intimidate her.
Spoil the plans of other girls who are trying to create fear and
isolation. Preserve my daughter's friendships and reputation—
don't let any gossip take hold to bring her shame.

Give my daughter's teachers and other parents the insight
and strength to stand up for my daughter. Bring about justice
for her; bring every secret into the light and let the truth be
clear.

Redeem what has been lost for my daughter. If she has lost
confidence, renew her motivation and strength. If friendships
have been torn apart, bring forgiveness and unity. If fear has
taken hold, give her courage to face each new day, knowing you

are with her. If she is beginning to believe their hateful words, remind her that she is yours—a beloved child of the living God.

Give my daughter compassion for those against her. Keep her from retaliating with anger or gossip. Help her to pray for them, to forgive, and not to take revenge in any form.

Use this struggle to reveal your power to my daughter. Grow her faith and trust as you come to her rescue. Thank you for the hope and protection we find in you. You are good! Amen.

– 60 –

When She Connects with Her Mom

Be completely humble and gentle; be patient, bearing with one another in love. Make every effort to keep the unity of the Spirit through the bond of peace.

Ephesians 4:2–3

Love is patient, love is kind. It does not envy, it does not boast, it is not proud. It does not dishonor others, it is not self-seeking, it is not easily angered, it keeps no record of wrongs. Love does not delight in evil but rejoices with the truth. It always protects, always trusts, always hopes, always perseveres. Love never fails.

1 Corinthians 13:4–8

Lord,

I pray for your hand over my daughter's relationship with her mom. As she grows and matures, so many issues can arise that create tension between them. As my daughter moves to greater independence and individuality, she may resent her mother's influence. The love between them can get lost in conflict.

It's impossible to expect my daughter and her mom to agree about everything all the time. Their opinions about fashion, dating, free-time activities, friends, spending habits, and household chores can clash and drive a wedge between them. Help them to remember that it's not about winning—let compassion and understanding be first in their minds.

Guard them from becoming caught up in a power struggle. Give my daughter a submissive heart so she can accept the limits necessary for her protection. Give her mom wisdom to know when to release control. Allow her mom to celebrate her daughter's initiative instead of just grieving the loss of her once-little girl.

When conflict happens, keep all bitterness and resentment from taking hold. Help them to forgive and move forward. Allow them to remember what they value in each other so they don't fall into negativity.

Mark their relationship with patience and self-control. Help them to choose their words carefully even when they're angry. Don't allow them to tear each other down. Remind them that today's frustrations will pass and tomorrow is a new day!

Preserve their hope in each other. When moods are sinking and understanding seems impossible, give them the courage to pursue peace until it's found. Keep them on each other's side. Give them assurance of each other's love no matter how challenging things seem at the time.

Use me as a blessing in their relationship. Give me wisdom to know when to step in to a conflict and when to stand by quietly and pray. Help me to honor my daughter's mother as an example of respect. If my daughter resists her mom's instruction, give me the strength to uphold the authority in our home. Teach me how to encourage both of them in forgiveness and compassion.

Thank you for giving them to each other. May they walk by your Spirit in the days ahead. Amen.

– 61 –

When We Need Time Together

Be very careful, then, how you live—not as unwise but as wise, making the most of every opportunity, because the days are evil. Therefore do not be foolish, but understand what the Lord's will is.

Ephesians 5:15–17

There is a time for everything, and a season for every activity under the heavens: a time to be born and a time to die, a time to plant and a time to uproot, a time to kill and a time to heal, a time to tear down and a time to build, a time to weep and a time to laugh, a time to mourn and a time to dance, a time to scatter stones and a time to gather them, a time to embrace and a time to refrain from embracing, a time to search and a time to give up, a time to keep and a time to throw away, a time to tear and a time to mend, a time to be silent and a time to speak.

Ecclesiastes 3:1–7

Lord,

Although you are eternal, you "teach us to number our days that we may get a heart of wisdom" (Ps. 90:12 ESV). We are so conscious of how fast time flies by. It seems like yesterday that my daughter was born, then learned to walk and talk, and now she is moving toward adulthood in the blink of an eye.

It would be so easy to squander these years with her as a child in my home. I'll often put off having special time with her, thinking, *It can wait until next weekend. Or next summer. Or next year.* I'll collect books I'd like to read with her, but they sit on the shelf. I imagine projects we could work on together, but the tools gather dust. A daddy-daughter dance sounds fun but doesn't make it onto the calendar.

Wake me up, Lord, with a sense of urgency about how short our days are together. Prompt me to pursue my daughter's heart with all my strength. Help me to shut out the distractions that keep me from spending time with her and really listening to what she has to say. Keep us from making commitments to others before I consider the impact they will have on my ability to parent her wholeheartedly.

This is my time to plant, build, laugh, embrace, dance, and speak into my daughter's mind and heart. Help me to make the most of every opportunity to share your Word and your love with her. You have given me the privilege of raising this precious girl—keep me from foolish thinking that says I can do that just by fitting her around the edges of my life.

Thank you for the time I've been given with my daughter. Each year has been a gift. The memories we've created are priceless treasures. May the times ahead be even more rich and blessed than what we've known so far. Amen.

– 62 –

When She Feels Pressure to Achieve

Am I now trying to win the approval of human beings, or of God? Or am I trying to please people? If I were still trying to please people, I would not be a servant of Christ.

Galatians 1:10

What do people get for all the toil and anxious striving with which they labor under the sun? All their days their work is grief and pain; even at night their minds do not rest. This too is meaningless. A person can do nothing better than to eat and drink and find satisfaction in their own toil. This too, I see, is from the hand of God.

Ecclesiastes 2:22–24

Whatever you do, work at it with all your heart, as working for the Lord, not for human masters, since you know that you will receive an inheritance from the Lord as a reward. It is the Lord Christ you are serving.

Colossians 3:23–24

Father,

You know the pressure on my daughter to succeed. She's constantly being measured and evaluated for her success at school and outside activities. There's always a new bar to reach for, another test of her skill, one more competitor to beat.

Ease my daughter's mind with the assurance that *you* are the only one she needs to please. Release her from the performance trap that says she has to be the very best—that her worth is determined by the judgment of other people. I see her knotted up with anxiety about her grades and other activities, with a doubting voice in her mind saying, *You might not be good enough.*

Help her to see that any success or award will fall away in the end. The only real rewards are those from you, and they will endure forever. Prompt her to develop higher goals of loving more, serving more, and becoming more like Christ. When she works at a task, energize her with the knowledge that she is fully accepted by you and she can tackle a challenge with joy.

Give my daughter peace in living for you rather than striving to please others. Allow her to find rest in your love. You give her grace and say that "my yoke is easy and my burden is light" (Matt. 11:30).

Thank you for the comfort we find in your mercy. Reveal yourself to my daughter so she can work at all things with joy and freedom. Amen.

- 63 -

When She's Choosing Who to Worship

Those who cling to worthless idols turn away from God's love for them.

Jonah 2:8

And the Levites . . . said: "Stand up and praise the LORD your God, who is from everlasting to everlasting." "Blessed be your glorious name, and may it be exalted above all blessing and praise. You alone are the LORD. You made the heavens, even the highest heavens, and all their starry host, the earth and all that is on it, the seas and all that is in them. You give life to everything, and the multitudes of heaven worship you."

Nehemiah 9:5–6

Among the gods there is none like you, Lord; no deeds can compare with yours. All the nations you have made will come and worship before you, Lord; they will bring glory to your name. For you are great and do marvelous deeds; you alone are God. Teach me your way, LORD, that I may rely on your faithfulness; give me an undivided heart, that I may fear your name.

Psalm 86:8–11

Lord God,

We are continually tempted to devote ourselves to what we can see with our eyes. Instead of giving all our praise to you, we love the things you have made instead. We create idols out of our blessings instead of giving you our gratitude.

Help my daughter to keep you first in her heart. You've given her beauty—keep her from vanity that fixates her mind on clothes and makeup. You've given her a full pantry and refrigerator—keep her from an unhealthy relationship with food. She has intelligence and abilities—keep her from finding her heart's satisfaction in awards and success. She has a room full of possessions—keep her from materialism and finding joy in accumulating more and more. She enjoys celebrities and artists—keep her from idolizing them since their talent and success are gifts from you. You've blessed her with wonderful relationships—let her desire to please *you* and enjoy your presence the most.

Lord, if she falls in love with people and pleasures of the world, she'll miss out on the wonder of you. No person or thing could ever match the power, love, and grace that you are ready to give. You offer eternal hope. Redemption. Freedom. Truth. Don't let her give her heart to anything or anyone but you.

May you always be my greatest desire. Let me be devoted to you, willing to forsake everything to follow you. Use me as an example of faith as I save my deepest praise, worship, and love for you alone.

Thank you for showing us the way. May your name be made great in all the earth! Amen.

Her Idols

Every one of us is, even from his mother's womb, a master craftsman of idols.

John Calvin[8]

One characteristic of idolatry is that it always confuses the creature with the creator.

Erwin Lutzer[9]

You don't have to go to heathen lands today to find false gods. America is full of them. Whatever you love more than God is your idol.

D. L. Moody[10]

All of us choose something to bow down to and to serve. As Augustine said, "Our hearts are restless until they rest in you." In the Old Testament we read about images made of wood, gold, and stone, temples and sacrifices and priestesses. But even then idolatry had more to do with the heart than any exterior rituals. Colossians 3:5 sheds light on this idea when God says to "put to death, therefore, whatever belongs to your earthly nature: sexual immorality, impurity, lust, evil desires and greed, which is idolatry." When we find ourselves "greedy," craving something to satisfy our hearts outside of God himself, then we have created an idol.

Our daughters need us to pray about what they worship. We live in a country where supposedly everyone is chasing the American Dream. So many of us pursue education, a career, and a house with two kids and a dog, hoping to feel satisfied. Our daughters are told from toddlerhood that if they work hard in school and pursue the most lucrative career they can find, they'll have all their hearts desire. We can even chart a certain course for them starting in preschool to guarantee their academic success. That doesn't leave much room for God's leading in their lives!

It's hard to say what the idols of my daughter's heart may become. Chances are they'll be related to her insecurities. If she thinks she needs to be beautiful to be happy and accepted, she'll make an idol of clothes, makeup, exercise, and primping in the bathroom! If she thinks that athletic success will make her significant, she'll practice for hours every week and be devastated if she loses a game. If she thinks that attracting boys will prove her worth, she'll flirt and even compromise her purity to hold their attention. Unless she believes she is completely accepted by God and can meet all of her needs in him, she'll never stop searching for peace.

I also need to pray for sensitivity to my daughter's struggles and needs. Sometimes I'm clueless that she's feeling lonely or insecure. I'm not at school with her all day, so I don't know who is bullying her, tempting her, or tearing her down. I'm not always aware that her great accomplishments are leading her into pride and self-sufficiency. Thankfully, if I need wisdom I can ask God, "who gives generously to all without finding fault" (James 1:5), and he promises to answer.

In the Old Testament the Israelites were tempted to run after idols when God didn't show up the way they wanted him to. In Exodus, when Moses went up on the mountain to receive the Ten Commandments, the Israelites wondered what was taking so long! By the time he came down the mountain they had melted down their jewelry and made a golden calf. We need to pray for endurance for ourselves and our daughters, to patiently wait on God to move in our lives. If my daughter is anxious for love, she'll need his help to wait for just the right godly man to marry. If she's battling an illness or injury that's keeping her isolated from her friends, it will take faith to wait for his healing. When the money runs out but the bills keep coming, only God can give us rest while we wait for his provision. We need faith to trust that he'll meet our needs in his way, in his perfect timing.

Another thing that always seemed to cause the Israelites' hearts to wander was the company they kept. God made it clear that he wanted his people to be set apart from the nations around them. He gave them unique laws to live by and his very presence in their midst. When they would disobey by intermarrying with other nations or becoming jealous of pagan religions, they would be led astray every time. Our daughters can experience that too, when they forget they are set apart by God. If their closest friends and influences are unbelievers, it will be next to impossible to stay strong in their faith. God gave us a wise warning when he said, "Do not be yoked together with unbelievers. For what do righteousness and wickedness have in common? Or what fellowship can light have with darkness?" (2 Cor. 6:14). He's not encouraging a holier-than-thou attitude, but he's guarding us from drifting away from him.

Sometimes we simply don't want to accept God's authority in our lives. As my daughter grows, she craves more and more independence. She wants more freedom to choose her friends, her classes, and how she spends her time. Being told what to do can become irritating, and God's ways stop looking so attractive. She can believe the lie that he's all about rules and wants to spoil her fun. When God says no, or wait, it's because he loves us and knows what's best. As parents we know we have to set limits—too much candy and our kids will ruin their teeth. Playing in the street will jeopardize their safety. Letting them skip school means suspension and failing grades. Just like we set boundaries to protect our precious daughters, God wants to protect them too. Let's pray that our daughters can submit to the Lord. He can give them the humility and self-control to follow him. They can receive his truth that freedom is found in obedience. Establishing our own authority as fathers is crucial as well. Let's not compromise what we believe is right because we're afraid of conflict with our kids.

I know my daughter is watching me to see what I worship. What am I telling myself will make me happy? What do I think I'm entitled to? What do I believe makes me significant and valuable? What am I trusting in for security? The answer to those questions will tell me where my heart is. I need to seek the Lord continually so he can show me by his Spirit if anyone or anything is replacing him in my life.

May our families worship the Lord and him alone, for every day of our lives. Let this be the cry of our hearts:

> Sing to the Lord, all the earth;
> proclaim his salvation day after day.
> Declare his glory among the nations,
> his marvelous deeds among all peoples.
>
> For great is the Lord and most worthy of praise;
> he is to be feared above all gods.
> For all the gods of the nations are idols,
> but the Lord made the heavens.
> Splendor and majesty are before him;
> strength and joy are in his dwelling place.

Ascribe to the Lord, all you families of nations,
   ascribe to the Lord glory and strength.
Ascribe to the Lord the glory due his name;
   bring an offering and come before him.
Worship the Lord in the splendor of his holiness.
   (1 Chron. 16:23–29)

– 64 –

When She Needs to Abide in God

I am the true vine, and my Father is the gardener. He cuts off every branch in me that bears no fruit, while every branch that does bear fruit he prunes so that it will be even more fruitful. You are already clean because of the word I have spoken to you. Remain in me, as I also remain in you. No branch can bear fruit by itself; it must remain in the vine. Neither can you bear fruit unless you remain in me. I am the vine; you are the branches. If you remain in me and I in you, you will bear much fruit; apart from me you can do nothing.

John 15:1–5

Let us hold fast the confession of our hope without wavering, for he who promised is faithful.

Hebrews 10:23 ESV

Father,

My daughter can be so easily distracted by her daily concerns that it's hard for her to stay close to you. Just like all of us, she can try to live by her own strength and figure out life by herself. She's tempted to set her own standards for right and wrong. She looks for truth and knowledge in the voices of people around her instead of your Word. She misses out on so many blessings and promises because she doesn't abide in you.

Help my daughter to know what it means to remain in you. Keep her near through prayer—let her share every detail of her days with you, and let her hear your Spirit's voice as he counsels her along the way. Make your Word come alive so she receives it and lives by its truth. Teach her spiritual discipline to meet with you daily so she can be transformed more and more into your likeness.

Lord, allow my daughter to "bear fruit," growing in love and goodness. Do your work in her life so that she becomes more and more like Jesus and develops humility, a servant's attitude, a spirit of joy and cheerfulness, generosity, kindness, self-control, and all of the other wonderful qualities that set apart a child of God.

Bind my daughter to you all the days of her life. Keep her from wandering onto paths that lead only to sin and pain. Write your Word on her heart so that your truth is with her continually. Give her discernment to recognize your voice when you speak.

Keep us faithful as you are faithful to us. Give us endurance to remain in you until we see you face-to-face. Amen.

– 65 –

When She's Growing in Maturity

When I was a child, I talked like a child, I thought like a child, I reasoned like a child. When I became a man, I put the ways of childhood behind me.

1 Corinthians 13:11

Then we will no longer be infants, tossed back and forth by the waves, and blown here and there by every wind of teaching and by the cunning and craftiness of people in their deceitful scheming. Instead, speaking the truth in love, we will grow to become in every respect the mature body of him who is the head, that is, Christ.

Ephesians 4:14–15

Let perseverance finish its work so that you may be mature and complete, not lacking anything. If any of you lacks wisdom, you should ask God, who gives generously to all without finding fault, and it will be given to you.

James 1:4–5

Father,

Growing up is hard work! It demands more responsibility, more effort, more discipline, and more confusing decisions year by year. Sometimes my daughter gets tired and wants to stay as she is or even go backward in her maturity.

Help my daughter to embrace her future. Let her face new challenges with boldness instead of fear. Allow her to hold on to her childlike creativity and imagination but be able to put aside her play when she has responsibilities at hand.

Help my daughter to participate in her own development. Give her an eager mind to learn and hands that try new things. Let her find happiness in managing her own room and possessions, earning money for her savings account, and taking leadership in her classroom. Give her initiative to help out around the house without being asked and look for ways to serve others.

Give my daughter satisfaction in growing in her knowledge of you. Teach her the spiritual disciplines of regular prayer and Bible study. Help her to store up your Word in her heart so she lives by its truth in every situation.

Use me as an example of maturity to my daughter. Keep me from neglecting to serve my family and church so I can "play" with sports, entertainment, or video games. Keep me from childish thinking that demands quick gratification instead of endurance. Make me wise in handling your Word so I'm not led astray by fads of thought or false teaching.

Thank you for the good plans you have for my daughter. You already know the young woman she will become—the knowledge, talents, accomplishments, and beauty that even now you are cultivating in her life. Thank you for the privilege of watching her grow. Amen.

– 66 –

When She Has a Need

And my God will meet all your needs according to the riches of his glory in Christ Jesus. To our God and Father be glory for ever and ever. Amen.

Philippians 4:19–20

So do not worry, saying, "What shall we eat?" or "What shall we drink?" or "What shall we wear?" For the pagans run after all these things, and your heavenly Father knows that you need them. But seek first his kingdom and his righteousness, and all these things will be given to you as well.

Matthew 6:31–33

The LORD is good, a refuge in times of trouble. He cares for those who trust in him.

Nahum 1:7

Father,

You are faithful and always keep your promises. You've never abandoned us in times of trouble. You see all and know all, so nothing that happens to us is a surprise to you. Your ears are always open to our prayers, and you invite us to cast all our cares on you.

You know the need that my daughter is struggling with today. She worries, doubts, and is preoccupied, wondering how the solution will come. Show my daughter what a generous, loving Father you are! Grow her faith and trust in you by meeting her need at this time. Let her be still before you. Help her to wait patiently without doubting as you provide for her at the perfect time.

Hold me back from trying to be her source for everything she needs. Don't let me steal your glory by running out to solve every difficulty for her. Let me show restraint, encouraging her to pray to you and wait for your answer. Direct me so I know when to help and when to simply rest on your promise to provide.

In the waiting, give my daughter peace and contentment. Keep her from worry and fretting. Let her have joy in the anticipation of seeing you move in this situation. Give her an unshakeable belief in your goodness as she puts her trust in you.

Thank you for caring for us in every way. You set us free from despair and fill us with hope. You are our refuge and give us good things all the days of our lives. To God be the glory! Amen.

– 67 –

When She Needs Peace and Rest

Be still, and know that I am God; I will be exalted among the nations, I will be exalted in the earth.

Psalm 46:10

Come to me, all who labor and are heavy laden, and I will give you rest. Take my yoke upon you, and learn from me, for I am gentle and lowly in heart, and you will find rest for your souls. For my yoke is easy, and my burden is light.

Matthew 11:28–30 ESV

The LORD is my shepherd, I lack nothing. He makes me lie down in green pastures, he leads me beside quiet waters, he refreshes my soul.

Psalm 23:1–3

Father,

You know that my daughter and I can find ourselves overcome by stress. Our schedules can become packed with so many commitments that we never have a minute to breathe. Our responsibilities can feel like spinning plates, and if we relax for a moment something might fall apart. We can focus more on *doing* than *being*, and we forget what is truly most important.

Deliver my daughter from the frantic pace and stress she finds herself caught up in. Teach her to say no to merely good things to focus on the very best. Give me wisdom to know when to limit our activities so our family can connect to one another and to you.

Teach my daughter the art of being still. Help her to unplug and be quiet. Help her to recognize your still, small voice and keep her from drowning you out with busyness. Guard our home from too much "noise" so it can be a place of peace and rest.

Keep us from pride and from believing our hope rests in our own effort and striving. Let us trust fully in you, resting in the knowledge that you're all-powerful and in control of our future. Give us faith to trust in the work of Christ on the cross—let us rest in your grace and stop working to earn the love you've already given so freely.

Make me a man of steadiness and calm so I can be a source of peace for my daughter. May we pause each day to quiet our hearts before you and know your perfect rest. Amen.

– 68 –

When She Needs to Laugh

Our mouths were filled with laughter, our tongues with songs of joy. Then it was said among the nations, "The LORD has done great things for them." The LORD has done great things for us, and we are filled with joy.

Psalm 126:2–3

Rejoice in the LORD and be glad, you righteous; sing, all you who are upright in heart!

Psalm 32:11

But may the righteous be glad and rejoice before God; may they be happy and joyful. Sing to God, sing in praise of his name, extol him who rides on the clouds; rejoice before him—his name is the LORD.

Psalm 68:3–4

Father,

You have given us so many reasons to celebrate. We have a hope and future with you. We are delivered from our sins and given every spiritual blessing. We are set free from fear, doubt, and despair. You carry our burdens, comfort us when we hurt, and meet all of our needs. Your Word encourages us and helps us know what to do. We never have to walk through life alone.

Help my daughter to have a happy, joyful heart. Don't let day-to-day troubles steal her smile or make her forget all of your blessings. Give her eyes to see you and all the great and wonderful things you have done.

Bring fun into our family life. Make our home a place of laughter, free from complaining and negativity. Let the joy of our household spill over onto everyone who comes in, that they may have a taste of your goodness.

Help me to reflect your light in my tone of voice and demeanor toward my daughter. Keep me from taking minor issues too seriously and worrying over burdens that you will carry for me. Make me quick to laugh and ready to smile, and find humor to lighten my daughter's heart.

We rejoice in you and are glad, for you have done great things for us. Amen.

A Dad's Story

Recently, my daughter crossed the threshold between childhood and adulthood when she turned thirteen. Before me now stands a young lady where, seemingly moments earlier, had stood a little girl. While I know that I will always be her dad and will always have an influence on her life, I also realize the days of my greatest impact upon her character, values, and convictions are now past. For twelve years I tried to cultivate her spirit, hoping that the seed of faith would take root, but now the choice is hers. I will continue to nurture her, but the faith of her father must remain mine. Only she can make her faith her own.

> My [daughter], if you accept my words
> and store up my commands within you,
> turning your ear to wisdom
> and applying your heart to understanding—

indeed, if you call out for insight
> and cry aloud for understanding,
and if you look for it as for silver
> and search for it as for hidden treasure,
then you will understand the fear of the LORD
> and find the knowledge of God. (Prov. 2:1–5)

Steve Scott, founder of On Target Outfitters,
author of *Faith Afield: A Sportsman's Devotional*

– 69 –

When the Enemy Is Attacking

Be alert and of sober mind. Your enemy the devil prowls around like a roaring lion looking for someone to devour. Resist him, standing firm in the faith, because you know that the family of believers throughout the world is undergoing the same kind of sufferings.

1 Peter 5:8–9

Submit yourselves, then, to God. Resist the devil, and he will flee from you.

James 4:7

Finally, be strong in the Lord and in his mighty power. Put on the full armor of God, so that you can take your stand against the devil's schemes. For our struggle is not against flesh and blood, but against the rulers, against the authorities, against the powers of this dark world and against the spiritual forces of evil in the heavenly realms. Therefore put on the full armor of God, so

that when the day of evil comes, you may be able to stand your
ground, and after you have done everything, to stand.

Ephesians 6:10–13

Almighty God,

I look at my precious daughter and am filled with love for her. My every instinct is to cherish and protect her from every kind of harm. In every possible way I try to bless her as she grows. It's hard for me to comprehend that an evil enemy could be scheming against her, looking for ways to bring pain and destruction into her life.

Thank you that we don't have to live in fear of the enemy. You have given us your power and strength. Help my daughter to put on the full armor of God—your truth, righteousness, the gospel of peace, faith, salvation, and your Spirit—so she can stand her ground when the enemy rises up against her.

Give my daughter discernment to recognize the enemy's voice when he whispers lies in her ear. When he tells her she's a worthless failure, give her assurance that she's a precious child of God. When he tries to paralyze her with fear, give her courage and boldness by your power. When he entices her with temptation to sin, fill her with love for your ways. Show her that by resisting him in your great name, he will run away and she will stand victorious.

Keep my daughter close to you through prayer and your Word. Build her up in her faith so she can't be shaken. Use me as a warrior for her, continually bringing my daughter before you in prayer. You are mighty and able to save, and an ever-present help in trouble. Thank you for your amazing promises that give us peace and hope no matter how the enemy comes against us. Amen.

– 70 –

When She's Discovering
Her Spiritual Gifts

There are different kinds of gifts, but the same Spirit distributes
them. There are different kinds of service, but the same Lord.
There are different kinds of working, but in all of them and in
everyone it is the same God at work. Now to each one the mani-
festation of the Spirit is given for the common good.

1 Corinthians 12:4–7

Just as each of us has one body with many members, and these
members do not all have the same function, so in Christ we,
though many, form one body, and each member belongs to all
the others. We have different gifts, according to the grace given
to each of us. If your gift is prophesying, then prophesy in accor-
dance with your faith; if it is serving, then serve; if it is teaching,
then teach; if it is to encourage, then give encouragement; if it is
giving, then give generously; if it is to lead, do it diligently; if it
is to show mercy, do it cheerfully.

Romans 12:4–8

Father,

Thank you for creating a spiritual family that we can be a
part of as your children. You have blessed us through other
believers as we experience their encouragement, wisdom, help,
generosity, and teaching of your Word.

You have blessed each believer in Christ with gifts by your
Spirit. Thank you for equipping us to join in your work in this
world. You have enabled us to be and do so much more than
we could dream of in our own strength.

Give my daughter the joy of discovering her spiritual gifts.
Fill her with a love for your people, and show her the special
strengths you will provide for her to serve your church. If she's

musical, let her sing praises to you. If she has a heart for children, let her care for the little ones. If she can lead or teach, give her positions of influence. If she has compassion for the poor, let her give and share and prompt others to do the same.

Give me discernment to see your Spirit working in her life. If I see you prompting her to help, give, or encourage others, let me support her and set her free to follow your leading. Show me how to use my own spiritual gifts in the body of Christ so I can be an example to my daughter of serving and obedience.

Use her spiritual gifting as an assurance of your presence in her life. Let her trust in your power so she doesn't try to work in her own strength. Keep her humble when she sees your power enabling her to do wonderful things for others.

Thank you for allowing us to live out our faith with others who love you too. Amen.

– 71 –

When She's Critical of Others

Do not judge, or you too will be judged. For in the same way you judge others, you will be judged, and with the measure you use, it will be measured to you. Why do you look at the speck of sawdust in your brother's eye and pay no attention to the plank in your own eye? How can you say to your brother, "Let me take the speck out of your eye," when all the time there is a plank in your own eye?

Matthew 7:1–4

For by the grace given me I say to every one of you: Do not think of yourself more highly than you ought, but rather think of yourself with sober judgment, in accordance with the faith God has distributed to each of you.

Romans 12:3

Be completely humble and gentle; be patient, bearing with one another in love. Make every effort to keep the unity of the Spirit through the bond of peace.

Ephesians 4:2–3

Lord,

When you look at us, you choose to see Jesus in us instead of our sin and weaknesses. You declare us righteous. You give us new identities, such as *child of God*, *friend*, *witness*, *holy and beloved*, *God's temple*, and *light of the world*. We are overwhelmed by your mercy, that you overlook our failings and offer us complete acceptance and love.

Let us respond to your gift of grace with a humble spirit. Remind us that it is because of Christ's righteousness and not our own that we are declared perfect and holy. Let us care for others the way you do—with gentleness and patience.

Help my daughter to mind her own behavior and choices instead of judging everyone else's. It's easy to point fingers at the disrespectful student in her class, the girl whose hair and clothes are out of style, the kids with lower grades, and the ones who choose to have foul language and attitudes. Remind her that she too has spoken out of turn and disrespected her parents. She's had her own battles with rudeness, laziness, selfishness, and anger. We "all have sinned and fall short of the glory of God" (Rom. 3:23), and we're all lost without your salvation.

Keep a critical spirit from taking hold in our home. Let us use our words to affirm and build each other up. When one of us makes a mistake or struggles with our attitude, let us give forgiveness and understanding instead of putting each other down. Make our home a haven of grace where we accept one another just as we are.

Thank you for your patience with us. You bear with us even when we feel like we'll never overcome our sin. In you we have salvation and perfect peace, knowing you'll never give up on us or let us go. We praise your name for your mercy. Amen.

When She's Pressured to Fit In

Do not conform to the pattern of this world, but be transformed
by the renewing of your mind. Then you will be able to test and
approve what God's will is—his good, pleasing and perfect will.

Romans 12:2

Therefore be imitators of God, as beloved children. And walk
in love, as Christ loved us and gave himself up for us, a fragrant
offering and sacrifice to God.

Ephesians 5:1–2 ESV

Father,

It's so hard for my daughter to resist the pressure to fit in.
She feels like she has to dress just like her friends, listen to the
same music, and like the same movies. She wants to be unique
enough to feel special but not so original that she draws negative attention to herself.

She's at that stage of life where she's discovering who she is.
She tries out different looks and mannerisms and waits to see
how others respond. Sometimes her goal doesn't seem to be
finding her own true self that you've created but just finding
out what will bring the most acceptance from others.

Help my daughter to conform herself to your ways. Give
her a heart to imitate you—your kindness, justice, strength,
and goodness—rather than modeling herself after the pattern
of the world.

Transform my daughter by renewing her mind. Give her
eyes to see you working in her life and ears to hear your truth.
Fill her with your love so that loving others will motivate all of
her words and behavior. When girls are rejecting a new student
or shutting someone out of the group, let your love make her
friendly and accepting. When she's shopping for a new dress,

draw her to what's modest and lovely. When she's tempted to join in bad-mouthing the teacher, let her be respectful. When her friends resist their parents and reject their influence, keep my daughter's heart open and devoted to me.

Thank you for giving us a new life in you. We don't have to be trapped in the ways of the world but can experience freedom in Christ. Help us to remember each and every day that we are yours. Amen.

Her Gifts and Talents

Since you are an intentional creation of God, this means you don't create your life's mission, you discover it! When you adopt this perspective, life becomes a journey of discovery, an adventure into meaning and personal mission.

Reggie McNeal[11]

Therefore, I urge you, brothers and sisters, in view of God's mercy, to offer your bodies as living sacrifices, holy and pleasing to God—this is your true and proper worship. . . . For just as each of us has one body with many members, and these members do not all have the same function, so in Christ we who are many form one body, and each member belongs to all the others. We have different gifts, according to the grace given to each of us. If your gift is prophesying, then prophesy in accordance with your faith; if it is serving, then serve; if it is teaching, then teach; if it is to encourage, then give encouragement; if it is giving, then give generously; if it is to lead, do it diligently; if it is to show mercy, do it cheerfully.

Romans 12:1, 4–8

Every believer has gifts and talents that God has graciously blessed them with. It's exciting to see those abilities come to light in my daughters as they grow. I know I was feeling excited and proud when my oldest daughter performed a solo in the winter choir concert at school. It was great to see my youngest daughter's writing assignments receive admiration from her teacher. It does my heart good to see my middle daughter reaching out to the special-needs students at her school. Every dad feels that sense of satisfaction when he sees his daughter's talents taking shape before his eyes.

I love praying for my daughters in this area. I celebrate how God has made each of their personalities unique. If you have more than one child, you've probably scratched your head wondering how children coming from the same parents can be so different from one another! It confirms that they are the handiwork of God—if we were the ones creating them, they would be cookie-cutter similar and we'd make them just like us! It's important to keep in mind that God is the source of their interests, gifts, and abilities. He's the one who gives them the desires of their hearts (Ps. 37:4) and who will finish the work of making them who they are designed to be (Phil. 1:6).

It's amazing that we dads are included in the work God is doing in our daughters' lives. We get the privilege of discovering all the wonderful qualities he has made. We share in their adventures as they try new things. We get to provide support for them to grow their talents and find opportunities to use them. When we pray for our girls, we can ask him for guidance in how to foster confidence as they take on new challenges. We can remind them that they're special in God's eyes when they feel inferior. He can show us how to help in concrete ways—providing lessons, coaching teams, purchasing craft supplies—so they can develop their gifts wholeheartedly.

Through prayer I can ask God to guard my daughter's heart. When she is tempted to work for her own achievement and glory, he can reveal how she can use her gifts for him. He intends us to serve and bless one another with the abilities we're given, not use them to impress other people and find our own gain. It's important that I set an example in my own life. When I serve, am I looking for gratitude from other people? Do I work hard at my job just to impress my boss and make more money? Am

I more interested in drawing attention to myself, or to the One who created me? If my daughter sees a humble, giving heart in me, she'll be encouraged to care for others too.

My daughter lives in a world that tries to define her by her success. We idolize entertainers and watch TV shows that show off the lifestyles of celebrities. It seems like girls play "rock star" more than they play house these days. Girls are told their value comes from their beauty and achievements instead of the fact that they're created by God himself. I can help my girl to remember the source of her gifts by continually pointing her to the Lord. When she wins the game or gets the part in the play, I can lead her in prayers of praise for what God has enabled her to do by *his* strength.

I can also encourage my daughter by reminding her God made her unique in order to bless her. That can be hard for the girl who's been given academic ability when other kids call her a nerd or the teacher's pet. Or for the child who is taken advantage of for her generous heart that makes her love to share with others. If my daughter has been given an extra measure of compassion for the outcast, she can find herself shut out by the popular group. My daughter may need courage to exercise her gifts when they aren't valued by others around her. I can walk beside her, continually reminding her to trust God while he reveals his purposes for her life.

I have to pray for God's help to relinquish control in my daughter's life. I can become caught up in *my* dreams for her instead of placing her future fully in his hands. If our interests and personalities are opposites in certain ways, I need to give my daughter freedom to be herself. That means holding back from pushing her into activities that I enjoy. Validating her as she is instead of criticizing her personality. And cheering her on even if ballet recitals put me to sleep! I love that I can run to the Lord in prayer when I'm losing sight of how unique and wonderful she really is.

Celebrate your daughter as a creation of God. She is fearfully and wonderfully made; I know that full well (Ps. 139:14).

– 73 –

When She's Discontent

*I know what it is to be in need, and I know what it is to have
plenty. I have learned the secret of being content in any and every
situation, whether well fed or hungry, whether living in plenty
or in want. I can do all this through him who gives me strength.*

Philippians 4:12–13

*Rejoice always, pray continually, give thanks in all circum-
stances; for this is God's will for you in Christ Jesus.*

1 Thessalonians 5:16–18

*This is the day that the LORD has made; let us rejoice and be
glad in it. . . . Oh give thanks to the LORD, for he is good; for his
steadfast love endures forever!*

Psalm 118:24, 29 ESV

Lord,

We're so quick to complain and wish for what we don't
have. My daughter wants it to be summer when she's working through a pile of homework but misses the school year
when summer feels long and boring. She frets over wanting
new clothes but then can't find just the right outfit to please
her at the mall so she goes home empty-handed. A young
woman may worry if she'll ever find "the one" but then find
all kinds of things to complain about when a boyfriend does
come along.

Keep my daughter from a negative outlook, where life never
measures up to her expectations. Develop in her a grateful heart
so she can count her many blessings every day. Give her an ap-
preciation for her family, her home and school, her friends, and
her many material possessions. Give her a keen awareness of

her marvelous life—that she's spared from hunger, fear, and violence when so many girls around the world are suffering.

Lord, even when we struggle or have to do without, your goodness to us never fails. We don't always understand why things happen, but we can trust in your perfect plans because you promise to work everything for our good. We find comfort in knowing that your love for us endures forever. Draw my daughter to you, that she will pray continually and find that you will give her strength in every situation.

May we rejoice in each new day, knowing that you will be with us every hour. You have blessed us beyond what we can measure. Everything we have is a gift from you, and the gifts just keep coming. You are good and deserve all our praise forever. Amen.

– 74 –

When She Doubts Her Worth

But you are a chosen people, a royal priesthood, a holy nation, God's special possession, that you may declare the praises of him who called you out of darkness into his wonderful light.

1 Peter 2:9

Are not five sparrows sold for two pennies? Yet not one of them is forgotten by God. Indeed, the very hairs of your head are all numbered. Don't be afraid; you are worth more than many sparrows.

Luke 12:6–7

Lord,

My daughter's confidence is shaken. She has experienced failure when despite her best efforts she didn't reach the mark. She feels as if she doesn't quite fit in—she's shy and feels awkward in a group. She's becoming more aware of her own sinful faults. She is discouraged that she doesn't always measure up to her own values, much less the standards I teach her to live by.

She's beginning to wonder if she's good enough. She doesn't feel unique or special. Sometimes she wonders if she's invisible. She thinks she'll never overcome her weaknesses. She's afraid she'll be rejected by other girls when she doesn't fit in, by me when she's disobedient, and even by you if she falls into sin.

Give my daughter a full assurance of your love. May she be convinced of her great value in your sight. Not only do you know every detail about her but you also created her for a purpose and have chosen her to be your child. Give her eyes to see the unique qualities you've created that set her apart. Encourage her in knowing that the girl she is today will grow and change and that when she's older she'll be amazed at who you've created her to be.

Strengthen her with the knowledge that she is secure in your love and mine. Remind her that you have declared her righteous through the work of Christ—she doesn't have to earn your favor by being perfect. Nothing that she does or doesn't do could ever turn you away.

Show me how to encourage her. May my words express how much I enjoy and cherish her. Let me praise you continually for the gift she is, and may she know without a doubt how much she is treasured. Thank you for making her a princess—the priceless daughter of the King. Amen.

– 75 –

When She Tries to Be Perfect

But God chose the foolish things of the world to shame the wise;
God chose the weak things of the world to shame the strong.

God chose the lowly things of this world and the despised things—and the things that are not—to nullify the things that are, so that no one may boast before him. It is because of him that you are in Christ Jesus, who has become for us wisdom from God—that is, our righteousness, holiness and redemption. Therefore, as it is written: "Let the one who boasts boast in the Lord."

1 Corinthians 1:27–31

But he said to me, "My grace is sufficient for you, for my power is made perfect in weakness." Therefore I will boast all the more gladly about my weaknesses, so that Christ's power may rest on me. That is why, for Christ's sake, I delight in weaknesses, in insults, in hardships, in persecutions, in difficulties. For when I am weak, then I am strong.

2 Corinthians 12:9–10

Lord,

You and you alone are perfect! You are all-knowing and all-powerful. You are holy, and justice is in your hand. Your Word holds absolute truth. Your wisdom is always right, and your works are without compare. Your ways are higher than our ways—we can't begin to comprehend how truly wonderful you are.

My daughter is trying to take hold of perfection herself. I see her becoming trapped in the pressure to always succeed, win at everything, and never make a mistake. She never wants to be at fault or lose the good opinion of anyone. This pressure is exhausting and is draining her life. She has no peace because she thinks if she relaxes her efforts for a moment, she'll fail. Her smile is fading with her hope.

Lord, you never stop working in us to make us more like Christ. You are fully aware of our weakness but give us strength to overcome. Let my daughter run to you for mercy and help in every situation. Change her perspective so she desires *your* glory to be revealed in her life. Give her spiritual understanding to see that you move through her weakness, not her power. Let her declare your wonderful work in her life. When she is successful or overcomes a challenge, let her praise *you* for enabling it to be so. Give her a grateful heart for all that you do on her behalf.

Keep me from holding my daughter to an unrealistic standard. Don't let me expect more than she can give or maturity beyond her years. Keep me from using her success to promote my own image to others. Give me a gentle, compassionate heart to accept her just as she is. Make me patient as she grows in your good time.

You transform us and make us new. Thank you for loving us as we are and promising that "he who began a good work in you will carry it on to completion until the day of Christ Jesus" (Phil. 1:6). We have the hope of perfection with you! Amen.

– 76 –

When I'm Losing Hope in My Daughter

Love is patient, love is kind. It does not envy, it does not boast, it is not proud. It does not dishonor others, it is not self-seeking, it is not easily angered, it keeps no record of wrongs. Love does not delight in evil but rejoices with the truth. It always protects, always trusts, always hopes, always perseveres. Love never fails.

1 Corinthians 13:4–8

Be completely humble and gentle; be patient, bearing with one another in love. Make every effort to keep the unity of the Spirit through the bond of peace.

Ephesians 4:2–3

Father,

My daughter seems to take two steps forward and one step back as she grows and matures. She has battled the same weakness and temptation for so long, and when I think she's finally overcome, she slips right back to where she was before. I'm disappointed and frustrated. I'm beginning to wonder if she'll ever change.

As I lose faith in her, it's weakening our relationship. She's wary of me, and I'm having difficulty finding warmth and affection. We don't know how to talk about this issue—it turns into just one more lecture from me with excuses and resistance from her.

Help me to bear with her, believing you will work in her life in your perfect timing. I want to love like you, putting the past behind and holding on to hope for the future. I need grace to accept her as she is with all her imperfections.

Give me your father's heart that desires to protect my child. Give me a perspective so I will want to guard her from sin for her good, not to satisfy my selfish expectations. Teach me how to come alongside and point her to your strength to overcome any challenge she's going through.

Restore the trust between us. Guard us from rudeness and words spoken out of anger. Give her assurance that I'm on her side. Humble me to remember that we're both sinners in need of your grace. Help us to forgive each other and restore peace between us.

Thank you for loving us perfectly so we know what love is meant to be. May I never give up on my daughter—may she always be sure she has my heart. And in this kind of lavish, constant love, may you be glorified. Amen.

– 77 –

When She Expresses Herself

How many are your works, LORD! In wisdom you made them all; the earth is full of your creatures.

Psalm 104:24

So God created mankind in his own image, in the image of God he created them; male and female he created them.

Genesis 1:27

Father,

You have revealed yourself to all mankind through what you have made. You are the Creator of the world and all its beauty. "The heavens declare the glory of God; the skies proclaim the work of his hands" (Ps. 19:1).

Since we are made in your image, you enable each of us to share in your creativity. My daughter's imagination and drive to build, draw, sing, and explore are gifts from you. Who knows what songs, architectural structures, books, recipes, sculptures, computer applications, or landscapes may come from her wonderful mind.

Fill my daughter with confidence to discover and create. Give her opportunities to experience different means of expressing herself. Show her how to share her emotions and ideas with others through the works of her hands. Teach her that she can worship you in countless ways—all that she makes can be offerings of love to you.

Show me how to encourage creativity in my daughter. Let me stop my busyness to give my full attention to her drawings, poems, and plays. Make me her biggest fan at every school program and concert. Help me to affirm her efforts and silence any hurtful criticism before it comes out of my mouth. Humble me to appreciate her childlike creations.

Give us the provision for any materials, lessons, instruments, or work space she needs. Show her what talents you've given her by your Spirit. Even when she's older and caught up in work and studies, keep her imagination alive.

Thank you for making this world and sharing its wonders with us all. And thank you for creating my daughter—her laughter, her beauty, her smile. She is an amazing gift from you. Amen.

– 78 –

When I Give Her Too Much

Keep falsehood and lies far from me; give me neither poverty nor riches, but give me only my daily bread. Otherwise, I may have too much and disown you and say, "Who is the LORD?" Or I may become poor and steal, and so dishonor the name of my God.

Proverbs 30:8–9

Do not be afraid, little flock, for your Father has been pleased to give you the kingdom. Sell your possessions and give to the poor. Provide purses for yourselves that will not wear out, a treasure in heaven that will never fail, where no thief comes near and no moth destroys. For where your treasure is, there your heart will be also.

Luke 12:32–34

Lord,

You say that fathers know how to give good gifts to their children (Matt. 7:11). I do find satisfaction in knowing that my daughter is well fed, dressed in warm, clean clothes, and safe in a comfortable home. I provide her with transportation to where she needs to go, stay attentive to her education, and make sure she has medical attention when it's needed.

However, when it comes to anything outside of her necessities, I can become confused. I'm not always sure if I'm blessing her or spoiling her! She can be hard to resist when she asks for something with those big, beautiful eyes and sweet smile.

Give me wisdom to know when to open my wallet and when to say no. Let me have discernment to know when enough is enough. Keep me from blessing her so richly that she never has to wait for anything she desires. Don't let me give her so much that she never knows the satisfaction of earning a reward through hard work.

Lord, I don't want to replace you in her life. If I'm her constant provider of every heart's desire, she'll never go to you in prayer and delight in seeing you respond. She'll never develop patience to wait on your perfect timing to meet her needs. She'll become so consumed with material things that she'll develop a greedy spirit and hate to share. Possessions will become her first love instead of you.

In the times that I struggle financially, I grieve more over her losses than my own. Give me confidence that you will use these circumstances to teach us gratitude and patience. Let these times develop compassion in our hearts for those who are suffering. Build our faith in you and your promises to provide and meet our needs.

Thank you for every single gift you have showered down on my daughter and me. May we seek your kingdom first—let us find our treasure in you and you alone. Amen.

A Dad's Story

Until one particular Tuesday in November, my daughter Grace had been having a good experience in her first year at school. She was in kindergarten and loving the adventure of meeting new people and learning new things. But that Tuesday morning, as Grace was in my office getting ready to go to school for an afternoon field trip, she began to complain that she didn't feel well and didn't want to go to school—even though she had no signs of sickness. When I told her that if she stayed home she would have to stay in bed all afternoon, she didn't blink. "That is fine," she said. It wasn't like Grace to want to stay in bed even if she was sick, so I asked if something had happened at school. "Yesterday on the playground at recess, no one wanted to play with me. I asked two different girls and they said no." I could feel the sadness in her voice.

My first instinct was to find those girls who wouldn't play and give them a piece of my mind. Of course, I knew that was wrong. My second instinct seemed better. "What if Mom went with you? Would you feel better about going?" Grace brightened up and said, "Oh yes!" But immediately, I felt a prompting in my spirit that actually my second instinct was not sufficiently better than the first, especially when my wife, Lisa, reminded me that she was taking care of our two youngest children that afternoon and couldn't go. It was then that I felt God telling me what I should have said in the first place. "What if I pray extra hard for God to be with you? Would you go then?" Grace agreed that if I would pray, she would go. We prayed together, and then she left.

That afternoon, I cancelled my meetings so I would have time to devote to praying just for Grace and her field trip. Earnestly and fervently, I prayed as if Grace's spiritual life hung in the balance. "God," I said, "I know there are times that we have to learn that not everything in life goes great just because we pray. But please not today. Today let Grace learn that you answer prayer. Please be with her in such an obvious way that it will build her faith and cause her to trust in you. I know that if Lisa had gone with her, or if I had gone with her, her trust would be in us. Now, Lord, you can cause her trust to be in you. You have promised that you will never leave Grace or forsake her. Now fulfill that promise in a powerful way so that she might know that you are real." I prayed those words over and over again during the time Grace was on the field trip.

When 3:25 p.m. rolled around, I made sure I was at the kindergarten door to pick her up.

"How was the field trip?" I asked with bated breath.

"It was great, Daddy! God really answered our prayers!" Grace replied.

Thank you, Lord.

Jim Samra, senior pastor of Calvary Church, Grand Rapids, Michigan; author of *The Gift of Church, Being Conformed*, and *God Told Me*

– 79 –

When She Needs to Love God with All Her Heart

Jesus replied: "'Love the Lord your God with all your heart and with all your soul and with all your mind.' This is the first and greatest commandment."

Matthew 22:37–38

Teach me your way, Lord, that I may rely on your faithfulness; give me an undivided heart, that I may fear your name. I will praise you, Lord my God, with all my heart; I will glorify your name forever.

Psalm 86:11–12

And now, Israel, what does the LORD your God ask of you but to fear the LORD your God, to walk in obedience to him, to love him, to serve the LORD your God with all your heart and with all your soul, and to observe the LORD's commands and decrees that I am giving you today for your own good? To the LORD your God belong the heavens, even the highest heavens, the earth and everything in it.

Deuteronomy 10:12–14

Lord,

Sometimes we can be satisfied with just a little bit of you. We are encouraged by the worship service on Sunday morning but show even more enthusiasm during Monday Night Football. We spend more time reading the headlines than reading your Word, even though it promises to change our lives! We say grace before meals but don't take time away to cry out to you on our knees and experience your presence.

Give us a heart to love you more than anything. Let us go "all in" with you, eager to obey you in all things, serve you with all our energy, and do everything for your glory. Turn my daughter's heart to you. Reveal yourself so she can see your power. Give her faith to believe you are her Creator, deserving all her worship and praise.

Keep my daughter from becoming devoted to lesser things. Her busy schedule can crowd out time with you. She can become more attached to other girls than her true Friend. She can be satisfied with just pleasing me instead of finding out *your* will and how you're asking her to obey. She can become more satisfied with her blessings than the One who is the source of all the good in her life.

We need your help to hold on to faith in what we can't see. May you be just as real to us as anyone we can see face-to-face. Help us to love you with all of our hearts so we can live for you without compromise. Own us, Lord, and keep us close to you forever. Amen.

- 80 -

When She Needs Compassion

My command is this: Love each other as I have loved you. Greater love has no one than this, to lay down one's life for one's friends.

John 15:12–13

A new command I give you: Love one another. As I have loved you, so you must love one another. By this everyone will know that you are my disciples, if you love one another.

John 13:34–35

Now that you have purified yourselves by obeying the truth so that you have sincere love for each other, love one another deeply, from the heart. . . . Finally, all of you, be like-minded, be sympathetic, love one another, be compassionate and humble.

1 Peter 1:22; 3:8

Father,

My daughter, just like every other person, has experienced hurt and pain. This world holds risk and danger. She will inevitably suffer the loss of loved ones to illnesses and tragic accidents. She may lose a job, a friend, or a dream she holds dear. She may be lied to, let down, and disappointed.

Thank you that even though we live in this broken world, you give us your comfort. In your wonderful plan you created a spiritual family for us to belong to. You have provided a haven from the darkness in the loving community of your people.

Help my daughter to experience real Christian love. Put caring people in her life who can be like Jesus to her. When she's lonely or feels she doesn't belong, help her to find friendship with other believers. If she's confused about a decision, let her find wise counsel. When she has a financial or material need, prompt a brother or sister in Christ to be generous and help her out. When something wonderful happens in her life, bring others close to celebrate with her.

Allow my daughter to be your light in the world. Use her humility, generosity, and compassion to give others a glimpse of you. Give her opportunities not just to encourage with her words but to give generously to others. Make her a peacemaker, quick to resolve conflict with others. Give her a forgiving spirit so she can show grace when others let her down.

When my daughter goes to school with stories of how her church has reached out to her, use it to draw kids to yourself. If our church isn't loving one another as you desire, give me the courage to lead the way by example. And if we must make a change and find a church family that is living out your will more fully, give me the wisdom to know where we should be.

Use the compassion of your people to fully convince my daughter of *your* love for her. Thank you for giving us a place to belong. Your kindness is beyond all we could hope or ask for. Amen.

– 81 –

When She Goes through Trials

Consider it pure joy, my brothers and sisters, whenever you face trials of many kinds, because you know that the testing of your faith develops perseverance. Let perseverance finish its work so that you may be mature and complete, not lacking anything.

James 1:2–4

Praise be to the God and Father of our Lord Jesus Christ! In his great mercy he has given us new birth into a living hope through the resurrection of Jesus Christ from the dead, and into an inheritance that can never perish, spoil or fade. This inheritance is kept in heaven for you, who through faith are shielded by God's power until the coming of the salvation that is ready to be revealed in the last time. In all this you greatly rejoice, though now for a little while you may have had to suffer grief in all kinds of trials. These have come so that the proven genuineness of your faith—of greater worth than gold, which perishes even though refined by fire—may result in praise, glory and honor when Jesus Christ is revealed.

1 Peter 1:3–7

Lord,

It's hard for me to sit by and watch my daughter struggle. I want to fix all her problems and shield her from any kind of pain. It's impossible, though, to spare her from the trials of life and I would be foolish to attempt it.

Give me faith to see that you have a purpose for the difficulties that come her way. Without any challenges, she can never learn to hang in there and overcome. She won't find that she can run to you and discover your wonderful deliverance. She'll miss out on the patience and faith that you want to develop in her heart.

When my daughter has an academic concept, athletic skill, or musical piece that she just can't seem to learn, give her the perseverance to keep working until she masters it. When a relationship is broken and communication seems impossible, bring forgiveness and understanding between them. When she's been fighting illness for a long time and never seems able to regain her strength, bring healing and energy to her body. When she gives in to the same temptation over and over, and thinks she'll never find the strength to resist, show her that you can give her all she needs to stand firm.

Reveal the wonderful mystery to my daughter that trials can be blessings in disguise. We discover how much we need you. We find hope and help in you that are beyond our expectations. We are transformed into people of strength and faith as we persevere until the difficulty has passed.

Use these hard times to build my daughter's trust in you. Use them to draw her near to you to discover your love. May she praise you for your goodness and thank you for every situation that shapes her into the girl you have created her to be. You are an amazing God—only you could take her pain and turn it into something beautiful. Amen.

Her Relationship with God

Model for your children that, more than just a worldview or a way of life, Christianity is first and foremost an intimate relationship with the Father.

Dr. Chap Clark and Dr. Kara E. Powell[12]

We must focus on Jesus, the source and goal of our faith. He saw the joy ahead of him, so he endured death on the cross and ignored the disgrace it brought him. Then he received the highest position in heaven, the one next to the throne of God.

Hebrews 12:2 GW

I have a lot of responsibilities as a dad: to provide, protect, teach, and love. But my absolute highest purpose is to introduce my daughter to God! Through my words and example, she needs to hear the truth of who he is and how much he loves her.

My greatest desire is for my daughter to place her trust in God. To understand the gospel message as it reveals the work of Christ and how she can be saved. To love the Lord with all her soul and mind and strength (Mark 12:30). Any other hopes I have for her are meaningless compared to knowing her Savior.

Thankfully it is the Lord who ultimately draws her to himself. I don't have the power to save her from her sins, but I can rest in knowing *he* is fully able to reach my daughter's heart. It encourages me that God hears my prayers for my daughter, whether I'm asking for her salvation or that he help her remain faithful in following him.

I also pray for help in living a godly life before her. She can see through any of my double standards, or if I'm just living to please myself. I pray I'll live in obedience in every area and surrender my life to God's control. I ask for help in staying diligent in my study of the Word so she'll know it is the source of my wisdom and values. God can help me serve others even when I'm tired. And he can give me unconditional love for my daughter that mirrors the perfect love he holds for her too.

In his book *Raising Kids Who Turn Out Right*, Dr. Tim Kimmel wisely said, "A child will not accept a life plan to which his parents only give mental assent. If a child is going to accept your faith as his own, he must see it lived out. Alive and breathing and functioning. In YOU!"[13] I pray continually that my walk with God will be about worship instead of just following the rules. I want my daughter to see authenticity, where what I say matches how I live. I ask that he will remain my true God so I don't fall away by loving the things of the world more than him.

God has some awesome promises for us! He says he "has blessed us in the heavenly realms with every spiritual blessing in Christ" (Eph. 1:3). And he tells me that "his divine power has given us everything we need for a godly life through our knowledge of him who called us by his own glory and goodness" (2 Pet. 1:3). Those verses encourage me so much when I'm feeling like a spiritual failure. They let me know that I have everything I need to parent my daughter. He gives me strength even when I feel inadequate.

Since God has given me all of those spiritual blessings, I'm excited to share them with my daughter! I can commit to a local church and place her in a body of believers who care for her. I can open the Word and study with her on a regular basis. Our "house rules" can reflect the perfect ways of God by encouraging kindness and respect. I can share God's grace with her by my forgiving spirit and never turning her away. We can enjoy worship together, praying and singing along with music in the car. We can find the joy of serving others as a family by helping those around us. I can enjoy God with her every time I say thanks for the good things he's doing for our family.

Perhaps your daughter is skeptical of the faith you've embraced for yourself. Maybe she's having trouble believing in someone she can't see. She could be having a hard time laying down her own desires to obey God's will. Satan can even put blinders over her mind and heart so it's harder for her to hear the truth of God. Maybe she asked Jesus into her heart as a little girl but is losing her commitment to live for him. Take comfort in knowing that God can reach her! Keep loving her right where she is. Keep following him faithfully. And know that your prayers do make a difference. "The prayer of a righteous person is powerful and effective" (James 5:16). Let's hold on to that promise as we continue to pray for our daughters and *never* give up.

– 82 –

When She's Feeling Guilty

Therefore, there is now no condemnation for those who are in Christ Jesus.

Romans 8:1

Therefore, brothers and sisters, since we have confidence to enter the Most Holy Place by the blood of Jesus, by a new and living way opened for us through the curtain, that is, his body, and since we have a great priest over the house of God, let us draw near to God with a sincere heart and with the full assurance that faith brings, having our hearts sprinkled to cleanse us from a guilty conscience and having our bodies washed with pure water. Let us hold unswervingly to the hope we profess, for he who promised is faithful.

Hebrews 10:19–23

I sought the LORD, and he answered me; he delivered me from all my fears. Those who look to him are radiant; their faces are never covered with shame.

Psalm 34:4–5

Father,

My daughter has sinned. She knew what she should do but her heart was set on having her own way. She was caught up in the moment and made the wrong choice. The consequences were painful and she feels ashamed that she went against her conscience when she knew what was right. She's doubting that she can be forgiven by you, because she just can't seem to forgive herself.

Give my daughter assurance of your grace. She confessed her sin, is committed to repenting by turning back to the right path, and knows that she has been forgiven by me. Give her faith to believe in Christ's work on the cross, that it paid the penalty for her sin and no other payment is required. You are not angry but look on her with compassion. You want to use this experience to reveal your kindness and make her more holy and perfect.

Convince her that you want to shape her character, not hand out punishment. You want her to rejoice in your salvation instead of dwelling on her shame. You want her to draw near to you with confidence rather than shrinking back in fear. Fill her heart with trust in your mercy and hope in her eternal future with you.

Make me like you as her father. When she disappoints me or lets me down, let me forgive without keeping a record of her failures in my mind. Keep me from dredging up memories of past mistakes to make her feel ashamed. Help me to quiet my frustrated emotions so I remain kind and approachable.

Keep me from anger that will drive her away, afraid to come to me when she's failed.

Thank you for promising to "remember their sins no more" (Heb. 8:12). You set us free from condemnation, make us clean and new, and invite us to come close to you. We love you and praise your name! Amen.

– 83 –

When She Compares Herself to Others

You, then, why do you judge your brother or sister? Or why do you treat them with contempt? For we will all stand before God's judgment seat. It is written: "'As surely as I live,' says the Lord, 'every knee will bow before me; every tongue will acknowledge God.'" So then, each of us will give an account of ourselves to God. Therefore let us stop passing judgment on one another.

Romans 14:10–13

Here there is no Gentile or Jew, circumcised or uncircumcised, barbarian, Scythian, slave or free, but Christ is all, and is in all. Therefore, as God's chosen people, holy and dearly loved, clothe yourselves with compassion, kindness, humility, gentleness and patience.

Colossians 3:11–12

Father,

Girls are so quick to notice who is the most popular in their school. They analyze each other's fashion choices. They compare to see who is the most overweight or thinnest. Who has the highest grades. Who has the latest technology and the most strict or lenient parents. Their minds are in a constant state of measuring how they stack up to everyone else.

It's so common for girls to try to boost themselves up by putting others down. They think if they can draw attention to the faults and quirks of other kids, it will make them look better by comparison. Or they become envious of the praise and attention given to someone else, so they criticize and make fun as a result of their own jealousy.

Defend my daughter from those who would cut her down. Give her confidence in your love and mine so she feels secure. Keep her from taking rudeness to heart by trusting in who you say she is—a King's daughter who was loved before the creation of the world. Remind her of her worth and the wonderful qualities you have woven into her mind and personality.

Give my daughter true friends who appreciate her just as she is. Keep them from a competitive spirit that causes them to try to outdo each other in everything. Humble their hearts to accept that every person is flawed in different ways. Give them compassion and kindness to reach out to girls around them with the gift of friendship.

Fill my daughter's heart with gratitude for your salvation. When she's tempted to feel superior to other girls in any way, remind her that we all have sinned and are lost without you. When she's insecure and feels inferior because other girls seem more talented or beautiful than she is, let her trust in your perfect love that never shows favoritism.

My daughter will stumble every time she compares herself to others. Let her judge her worth and actions by your standards alone. Give her a generous spirit so she can celebrate the good things she sees in those around her. Guard her mouth from critical words, and give her an open heart to accept people as they are.

Thank you for setting us free from the comparison trap. Thank you for accepting us and adopting us as your children. You make us new and give us hope for the future. We praise your glorious name. Amen.

– 84 –

When She Longs for Beauty

Charm is deceptive, and beauty is fleeting; but a woman who fears the LORD *is to be praised.*

Proverbs 31:30

Your beauty should not come from outward adornment, such as elaborate hairstyles and the wearing of gold jewelry or fine clothes. Rather, it should be that of your inner self, the unfading beauty of a gentle and quiet spirit, which is of great worth in God's sight.

1 Peter 3:3–4

For you created my inmost being; you knit me together in my mother's womb. I praise you because I am fearfully and wonderfully made; your works are wonderful, I know that full well.

Psalm 139:13–14

Father,

I know I'm biased but I think my daughter is the most beautiful girl in the world! I've been captivated ever since she was placed in my arms on the day of her birth. Her laughter and smiles are contagious, and I melt when she wraps her arms around me and says, "I love you, Daddy."

It hurts when I see her doubting how beautiful she is. I want her to believe she is special in every way. It's hard to see her worry and cry about her skin, her weight, and her wardrobe, and if she'll be accepted and fit in.

I want her to find rest from all her efforts to "fix" herself— shopping for clothes, questioning her diet, fixing her hair six different ways before she leaves for school in the morning. Sometimes I get angry, thinking she's just being vain and wasting time. I get frustrated that no matter how many clothes I buy, she doesn't have anything to wear! I wonder how she can spend an entire afternoon with her friends experimenting with nail polish and makeup.

Set my daughter free with the knowledge that true beauty is found in her inner self. No matter how much energy she spends on perfecting her appearance, she'll never overcome the effects of time. She can't control whether genetics made her tall or short. Accidents leave scars she is unable to hide. If she believes that her outer beauty is all that matters, she'll fall into discouragement and despair.

Fill my daughter with your Spirit. Teach her heart to value a gentle, peaceful attitude. A girl full of love and compassion is always the most beautiful girl in the room.

Remind my daughter that she is your creation. You have declared that she is wonderfully made. You designed every physical detail with love and care—she can rest in knowing she is exactly as she should be.

Use me to encourage her and love her well. Give me eyes to see what matters most. Let me affirm her inner qualities—her intelligence, caring spirit, humor, generosity—rather than focusing on her outer appearance. May I praise you continually for the lovely gift of my daughter. Thank you for the hope she can find in you. May she rest in your great love and find perfect hope as your child. Amen.

– 85 –

When She Needs to Hang In There

[And we pray this] so that you may live a life worthy of the Lord and please him in every way: bearing fruit in every good work, growing in the knowledge of God, being strengthened with all

power according to his glorious might so that you may have great endurance and patience.

Colossians 1:10–11

Let us not become weary in doing good, for at the proper time we will reap a harvest if we do not give up.

Galatians 6:9

In all my prayers for all of you, I always pray with joy because of your partnership in the gospel from the first day until now, being confident of this, that he who began a good work in you will carry it on to completion until the day of Christ Jesus.

Philippians 1:4–6

Lord,

My daughter is ready to quit! She's tired. She's frustrated. She's bored. She doesn't think her efforts are ever going to pay off. She thinks it's just too hard.

Use this situation to teach my daughter to persevere. She is so caught up in the moment that she can't see an end in sight. Give her a fresh burst of energy and confidence to keep on going.

You know the work she has to do. It's stretching her beyond what she thinks she's capable of. It's demanding that she rise above her doubts and weaknesses. Encourage her heart to know this challenge will bring her blessing if she takes it through to the end.

Let her see that she's not merely attempting to gain a prize, impress an audience, earn a grade, or hone her skills. You want to use this experience to transform her character. Let her discover you as Helper and grow in her knowledge of your power. Help her discover that you have rewards in mind that are amazing and will last forever.

Draw my daughter to you so she can lean on your strength. Develop the fruit of patience and endurance by your Spirit. Give her eyes to see past her circumstances to the spiritual work you are doing.

Use me as an encouragement. Keep me from pushy, critical words that will just bring her down. Don't let me speak a single word that sounds like *You'd better do it or else!* Make my optimism contagious and let me be her biggest fan.

Show my daughter that with you anything is possible. Increase her knowledge of you so she can love you more and more. We praise your name for your glorious might! Amen.

A Dad's Story

My oldest granddaughter is a dreamer. She is creative and confident and believes she has good plans for everyone. She thinks about scenarios ahead of time and plays them out in her heart before they even begin. Her ability to dream is so vibrant that it overwhelms her at times. She is often afraid of new opportunities because they have become so important in her heart. When it is time to engage she will resist, get embarrassed, or try to impose her will on a situation she cannot control. I have committed to pray that she learns to adjust to her gift and develop the skills that will help her appreciate her strengths.

She was excited the way only a five-year-old can be about her upcoming birthday party. When I showed up at the house she came running up to me and shouted, "Hi, Papa! I am going to have a birthday party, and we need to make invitations."

She handed me a stack of construction paper and a box of crayons. She announced the first name on her list and asked me to write out an invitation. She then ceremoniously rolled up the paper like a scroll and wrapped a decorative rubber band around our creation. We continued this process for twenty-five invitations, which I have to say were quite well done.

Being very proud of herself and her papa, she announced, "Okay, now we need to go to the post office and mail these." With that, she picked up her special bag of invitations and headed for the door. I admired her confidence, but it was happening again. Her dreams had gotten ahead of reality. In her heart, the plan was all figured out, and she expected it all to go according to plan.

I prayed, *Jesus, please give me wisdom on how to proceed with my precious granddaughter and help her learn to adjust her expectations to the reality of life.*

After praying, the first thought that came to mind was, *I need to tell her the truth.*

"Sweetie, we cannot take these invitations to the post office," I said. "These are personal invitations, and they need to be delivered in person."

The look on her face was astonishing. She was instantly disappointed and frustrated. You would have thought I had told her she was ugly or stupid. I could see the wheels of her mind whirling as I imagined what she must be thinking. *This can't be. Everything is ruined. These invitations are supposed to be mailed, and the mailman is supposed to deliver these to the houses. Now my friends won't get their invitations, nobody will come to my party, and I won't have a birthday. This is going to be the worst day of my life!*

I watched her agonize over this, but I knew I couldn't rescue her. I had to give her time to let her emotions catch up with the truth. She has a vibrant emotional makeup, so she will probably always struggle with her emotions lagging behind the decisions she must make.

It took about an hour this time, but she finally returned with a renewed look of hope and anticipation. "Papa, will you come to church with me this Sunday so we can hand these out to all my friends? I think they will all be there, and these are invitations we need to hand out personally."

I am now praying for her on a regular basis because I am confident it will be a lifelong struggle for her. I see natural leadership ability in her and an optimistic creativity. Her plans are so vivid, however, that they feel real to her as soon as she thinks about them. When they can't come true as she has envisioned, it will be a challenge. I am also praying that God will prepare a young man to be her future husband who has the ability to tell her the truth and then patiently wait for her emotions to catch up.

Bill Farrel, coauthor of *Men Are Like Waffles— Women Are Like Spaghetti, Red-Hot Monogamy,* and *The 10 Best Decisions a Couple Can Make*

– 86 –

When Her Reputation Is at Stake

A good name is more desirable than great riches; to be esteemed is better than silver or gold.

Proverbs 22:1

So do not fear, for I am with you; do not be dismayed, for I am your God. I will strengthen you and help you; I will uphold you with my righteous right hand. All who rage against you will surely be ashamed and disgraced; those who oppose you will be as nothing and perish. Though you search for your enemies, you will not find them. Those who wage war against you will be as nothing at all.

Isaiah 41:10–12

So we say with confidence, "The Lord is my helper; I will not be afraid. What can mere mortals do to me?"

Hebrews 13:6

Lord,

My daughter's reputation is threatened. Even though she has been diligent in doing the right thing, other people are questioning her integrity. They believe she's deceitful and manipulating the situation for her own best interest. No matter how much she tries to explain what's really going on, she can't convince everyone of the truth.

I pray that you would clear up this misunderstanding. Bring the facts into the light so my daughter's name can be cleared. Give everyone involved wisdom and discernment to know what to do and say. Give each person humility to admit any wrong and ask for forgiveness.

Guard my daughter's heart from bitterness toward her accusers. Keep her from anger or retaliation even though she's frustrated. Give her peace and grace to quietly continue doing what she knows is right. Use this situation to teach her patience—to wait on you for help instead of trying to fix it on her own. Protect her from discouragement until your work is complete.

Give me insight to know how to help my daughter. Let me keep our conversations centered on you and your promises instead of people's mistakes. If it's your will, provide opportunities for me to stand up for her. Let her know my faith in her is unshaken.

I pray that as you restore my daughter's reputation, you would also restore the relationships that are torn right now. Make my daughter a peacemaker through a gentle, forgiving spirit.

Use this experience to give my daughter compassion for others. Prompt her to stand up for others who need help. Give her courage to speak up for those who are being insulted or misunderstood. Make her the kind of person others can trust and rely on.

Thank you for your promises to help my daughter when she needs you. You are more powerful than anyone who can come against her. In you she can have courage instead of fear, peace instead of worry, and kindness instead of hatred. Amen.

When She Shows Favoritism

Rob and Joanna Teigen

My brothers and sisters, believers in our glorious Lord Jesus Christ must not show favoritism. Suppose a man comes into your meeting wearing a gold ring and fine clothes, and a poor man in filthy old clothes also comes in. If you show special attention to the man wearing fine clothes and say, "Here's a good seat for you," but say to the poor man, "You stand there" or "Sit on the floor by my feet," have you not discriminated among yourselves and become judges with evil thoughts? Listen, my dear brothers sisters: Has not God chosen those who are poor in the eyes of the world to be rich in faith and to inherit the kingdom he promised those who love him?

James 2:1–5

Do nothing out of selfish ambition or vain conceit. Rather, in humility value others above yourselves.

Philippians 2:3

Father,

From the time she was little, I've taught my daughter to share with other kids. I've trained her to say "please" and "thank you," and to let others go first. I've encouraged her to be a gracious winner and never a sore loser. She knows the Ten Commandments and the Golden Rule. She's aware that it's wrong to look down on others based on their race, looks, or handicaps.

All of these values are great but can be so difficult to practice when she's facing the threat of rejection at school. She's afraid that if she reaches out to girls who are left out, poor, or just *different*, she'll end up marginalized herself.

My daughter's friends might pressure her to stick with them when she's friendly to other girls. They might criticize by saying she's being self-righteous or acting superior or being disloyal. Girls who value their external image may look down on her if she lives by different priorities. She may end up feeling frustrated and misunderstood.

Give my daughter the courage to care for everyone. Guard her heart from pride. Keep her from showing favoritism. Make her responsive to your Spirit's prompting to reach out to those who are struggling. Give her eyes to see the value in every person no matter how different they seem on the outside.

Let my daughter set an example among her peers. As she shows grace and kindness, may her friends be inspired to do the same. Let her light shine before everyone so they see *your* love displayed. Use her as a living testimony of your goodness.

Let her be concerned with pleasing you instead of other people. Give her joy and satisfaction in living out her faith. Give her assurance of your reward when she pays a price for loving like Jesus.

Thank you for your wisdom that instructs us in your ways. I pray we would be your humble servants in every situation. Thank you for reaching out to *us* without showing favoritism—we can rest knowing we are fully accepted by you. We love you! Amen.

– 88 –

When She Needs the Word of God

All Scripture is God-breathed and is useful for teaching, rebuking, correcting and training in righteousness, so that the servant of God may be thoroughly equipped for every good work.

2 Timothy 3:16–17

How can a young person stay on the path of purity? By living according to your word. I seek you with all my heart; do not let me stray from your commands. I have hidden your word in my heart that I might not sin against you. Praise be to you, LORD; teach me your decrees. With my lips I recount all the laws that come from your mouth. I rejoice in following your statutes as one rejoices in great riches. I meditate on your precepts and consider your ways. I delight in your decrees; I will not neglect your word.

Psalm 119:9–16

Father,

You know my devotion to my daughter. I desire to teach her, guide her, and have influence in her life. I want to share the truth about you and help her to discover what a great God you are.

But my own efforts are weak and imperfect. I can't be her best source of wisdom or direction. The only way she'll discover perfect truth is from the Bible itself.

Place a deep longing in her heart for you! Make your Word come alive so she can receive all the gifts it contains—the message of salvation, your promises, encouragement, correction, knowledge, wisdom—for the treasures it holds are without number.

As a young person, she is still growing in devotion and discipline. Teach her to seek your truth every day. Give her the humility to ask for help when she doesn't understand. Fill her with courage to declare it as *your* Word even when the world dismisses it as a fable. Open her mind to comprehend mysteries that only your Spirit can reveal. Convict her. Lead her. Fill her with hope as she discovers its light for her path.

Make me a diligent student of your Word. Give me discernment to know how to "correctly handle the word of truth" so I can teach my daughter well (2 Tim. 2:15). May my faithfulness in spending time with you encourage her to pursue your Word.

Without hiding your Word in her heart, my daughter will be lost in sin and confusion. She'll never know the power it can bring to her life. She'll find herself ill-equipped to deal with stress or pain. She'll look for hope in useless places instead of in you alone. Let my daughter taste and see how sweet your words can be! When she holds your Book in her hands, may it be her greatest treasure.

Thank you for drawing near to us and revealing yourself through the Scriptures. Out of your amazing love you gave us everything we need for life and godliness. May we hold fast to everything the Bible teaches all the days of our lives. Make this our constant prayer:

> Oh, how I love your law!
>   I meditate on it all day long.
> Your commands are always with me
>   and make me wiser than my enemies.
> I have more insight than all my teachers,
>   for I meditate on your statutes.
> I have more understanding than the elders,
>   for I obey your precepts.
> I have kept my feet from every evil path
>   so that I might obey your word.
> I have not departed from your laws,
>   for you yourself have taught me.
> How sweet are your words to my taste,
>   sweeter than honey to my mouth!
> I gain understanding from your precepts;
>   therefore I hate every wrong path.
> Your word is a lamp for my feet,
>   a light on my path. (Ps. 119:97–105)

Amen.

Notes

1. Will Davis Jr., *Pray Big for Your Children* (Grand Rapids: Revell, 2009), 16.

2. Kevin Leman, *What a Difference a Daddy Makes: The Indelible Imprint a Dad Leaves on His Daughter's Life* (Nashville: Thomas Nelson, 2001), 5.

3. C. S. Lewis, *The Business of Heaven: Daily Reading from C. S. Lewis* (New York: Mariner Books, 1984), 22.

4. Mark Driscoll and Matt Smethurst, "Driscoll, Who Do You Think I Am?," *The Gospel Coalition Voices*, January 28, 2013, http://thegospelcoalition.org/blogs/tgc/2013/01/28/driscoll-who-do-you-think-i-am/.

5. Family Safe Media, "Pornography Statistics," accessed September 26, 2013, http://familysafemedia.com/pornography_statistics.html.

6. Christian Quotes, "Oswald Chambers," accessed September 26, 2013, http://christian-quotes.ochristian.com/Oswald-Chambers-Quotes/page-3.shtml.

7. Francis Chan, *Crazy Love: Overwhelmed by a Relentless God*, 2nd ed. (Colorado Springs: David C. Cook, 2013), 131.

8. John Calvin, *The One Year at His Feet Devotional* (Wheaton, IL: Tyndale Momentum, 2006), 24.

9. Erwin Lutzer, *10 Lies about God and the Truths that Shatter Deception* (Grand Rapids: Kregel, 2009), 89.

10. D. L. Moody, *Mornings with Moody* (Dallas: Primedia eLaunch, 2012), 36.

11. Reggie McNeal, *Get Off Your Donkey!: Help Somebody and Help Yourself* (Grand Rapids: Baker, 2013), 74.

12. Dr. Chap Clark and Dr. Kara E. Powell, *Sticky Faith: Everyday Ideas to Build Lasting Faith in Your Kids* (Grand Rapids: Zondervan, 2011), 65.

13. Dr. Tim Kimmel, *Raising Kids Who Turn Out Right* (Scottsdale, AZ: Family Matters, 2006).

Rob Teigen has been a publishing professional for more than fifteen years and is the author of three joke books, including *Laugh-Out-Loud Jokes for Kids* (under the pseudonym Rob Elliott). He and his wife, Joanna Teigen, are the parents of a teenage son and three younger daughters. They are the authors of *88 Great Daddy-Daughter Dates* and live in West Michigan. Find out more at www.strongerdads.com.

COMING
FALL 2014

A Mom's Prayers for Her Son
by Rob and Joanna Teigen

• • •

A practical guide for moms with
prayers for every area of her son's life

Revell
a division of Baker Publishing Group
www.RevellBooks.com

Start making memories that last a LIFETIME!

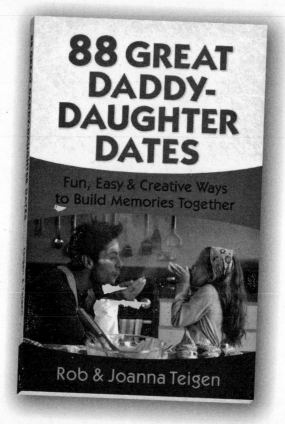

"If you want to capture the heart of your daughter, this book is a great place to start!"—Dr. Kevin Leman, *New York Times* bestselling author of *Have a New Kid by Friday*

"Wow! This book hits it out of the park. Finally, a straightforward tool that will equip dads to invest spiritually, love intentionally, and connect emotionally with their daughters."—Lysa TerKeurst, *New York Times* bestselling author of *Made to Crave*

To learn more, visit www.StrongerDads.com

Now, for the first time, all of ROB ELLIOTT'S popular joke books are in one hilarious volume.

Don't miss a moment of the fun and laughs!